BRIGHAM YOUNG.

LIFE AMONG

THE MORMONS,

AND

A MARCH TO THEIR ZION:

TO WHICH IS ADDED A CHAPTER ON THE INDIANS OF THE PLAINS AND MOUNTAINS OF THE WEST.

BY AN OFFICER OF THE U. S. ARMY.

NEW YORK:
MOORHEAD, SIMPSON & BOND.
1868.

Agathynian Press, 60 Duane Street, N. Y.

RESPECTFULLY DEDICATED

TO

Rev. JOHN P. NEWMAN, D.D.

(OF THE M. E. CHURCH,)

At whose suggestion this book was written, and

As a Mark of Respect to a Faithful Pastor,

A Warm Friend,

And a True Christian Gentleman,

Whose real worth, in these several capacities, has been fully appreciated and admired. His social relations are among the most pleasant memories of

THE AUTHOR,

While his ministerial duties and friendly sympathies will remain prominently associated with an event that will long cause pensive thoughts, but the recollection of which will the more firmly establish the most profound friendship.

INTRODUCTION.

Last spring I left St. Louis under orders of Major-General Pope, then commanding the Department of the Missouri, to accompany troops from that City to Camp Douglas, which overlooks the City of the Saints in the valley of the Great Salt Lake.

I started without any intention of writing a line descriptive of my journey, further than might be contained in my private correspondence; nor did I conceive the idea of preparing anything for publication until several weeks after the completion of my journey, when, in a letter from my friend, to whom I have inscribed this book, I was requested to furnish an account of my journey, and of the Mormons, for publication in the New Orleans *Advocate*, of which he is the editor.

I commenced a series of letters, with many misgivings as to my ability to make them entertaining or instructive. As the only record I kept of my experiences and observations was in a small pocket diary, I lacked the inspiration, which a record of scenes and events would have received if written about when they were observed or transpiring, and had to trust much to memory for incidents.

At the conclusion of the series my friend again comes forward and suggests their publication in book-form. Several other friends agreeing with him as to the fitness of things in doing so, I have relied upon their judgment more than upon my own, and compiled the letters for publication in their present form.

All the letters have been carefully revised, and some of them considerably elaborated, while those in which I attempted a history of the Mormons have been almost entirely rewritten and very largely added to.

It has been my fortune to have extraordinary opportunities of familiarizing myself with the practices and inner life of that strange people, and what I have herein recorded is no mere sensational narrative, to create a popularity for the work, but a plain statement of what I believe to be facts

I am not at liberty to mention the names of the parties from whom I received most of the information concerning the Mormons; but suffice it to say it was from those who spoke of *their own personal knowledge and observation.*

Having no aspirations for notoriety as an author, and having written these pages more for the gratification of my friends than for any advantage that can accrue to me individually, I would refer the reader to the Rev. Dr. Newman, as in a measure responsible for the publication, and I have no doubt, if he cannot indorse all that I have written, he will vouch for the honesty and disinterested motives of

THE AUTHOR.

Utah Territory, 1867.

CONTENTS.

CONTENTS.

CHAPTER IV.

CHAPTER V.

CHAPTER VI.

CHAPTER VII.

CHAPTER VIII.

PAGE

FROM GREEN RIVER TO FORT BRIDGER.

CHAPTER IX.

MORE ABOUT FORT BRIDGER.

CHAPTER X.

FROM FORT BRIDGER TO WANSHIP SETTLEMENT.

CHAPTER XI.

FROM WANSHIP TO SALT LAKE VALLEY.

CHAPTER XII.

CHAPTER XIII.

CHAPTER XIV.

PAGE

CHAPTER XV.

DOCTRINES OF THE MORMON CHURCH. POLYGAMY.

CHAPTER XVI.

PRACTICAL POLYGAMY.

CHAPTER XVII.

POLYGAMY CONTINUED.

CHAPTER XVIII.

WHERE THE MORMONS COME FROM AND HOW THEY REACH SALT LAKE.

CHAPTER XIX.

MORMON WORSHIP AND MORMON DIGNITARIES.

PAGE

CHAPTER XX.

CRIMES OF THE MORMONS AND HOW MORMONISM MAY BE ERADICATED.

CHAPTER XXI.

THE INDIANS OF THE PLAINS AND MOUNTAINS.

Life among the Mormons.

CHAPTER I.

FROM FORT LEAVENWORTH TO FORT KEARNEY.

FORT Leavenworth was, in April last, the grand rendezvous of troops of the regular army, who, as in former times, were to garrison posts on the frontier, whence they had been withdrawn in '61 to aid in suppressing the late great rebellion. From that point they were to proceed to the various forts North of the Arkansas, and as far West as Salt Lake City.

Outfits for several commands, as large as the one I accompanied, were furnished at Leavenworth; but so complete were the arrangements for meeting the demand, and so prompt the action in the different departments, that but little delay occurred, and, after camping only a few days in the vicinity, we struck tents and commenced our long Westward march.

The location of Fort Leavenworth is doubtless familiar to the reader. It is in Kansas, on the south bank of the Missouri, about 500 miles above its mouth, and overlooks the thriving city of the same name. It is one of the oldest military stations of the West, and has for many years been the depot from which supplies have been furnished the various posts on the plains.

It was my good fortune to accompany a detachment of the 18th U. S. Infantry, consisting of one battalion of eight companies, and recruits for two other battalions, numbering in all about 1300 men.

The whole was under the command of Major Van Voast, an experienced officer, long familiar with frontier life on the Pacific coast, and subordinate to him were a number of officers, belonging to the same regiment, who had proven their fitness for the positions they held by long and gallant services in the field with our Western armies. They were all strangers to me then; but three months of intimate, and constant association, caused a warm mutual friendship to exist, which will remain among the most pleasant memories of my army life.

But I must not in this connection neglect to refer to the most pleasant feature of the journey we were then about to commence. The presence of six ladies in our company, it is unnecessary to say, contributed largely to the enjoyment of the trip. Some of these ladies had campaigned with their husbands before, but the majority were then to experience life without the bounds of civilization for the first time. The latter class, however,—and among them were young ladies who had never been beyond the sound of a piano or a church bell,—appeared to enjoy the trip throughout more than those who were already familiar with the inconveniences incident to a journey of the kind. For our large command, with its attachés, on a long journey, no insignificant amount of transportation was required, and thanks to the obliging quartermaster, at Leavenworth, Col. Potter, our supply and baggage train was ample and numbered over 100 six mule army wagons, besides six ambulances, and the private conveyances of officers whose families accompanied them. There is something interesting connected with this train. The wagons that composed it had been sent overland the summer before from Washington, where they had been collected from the army of the Potomac after the close of the war. It was a singular coincidence to have with us on the march the same wagons that had followed us in the Peninsular campaign in '61, two thousand miles distant. That such was the case regarding some of them, our Quartermaster assured me there could be no doubt, for he recognized on several, marks which he had placed there when acting in the same capacity in the 5th army corps, during the eventful campaign referred to. A still more remarkable coincidence was that of a driver having in his team a span of mules which he said were, most unquestionably, the identical mules he had driven from the position our army held in front of Richmond to Harrison's Landing on the James River at the time of the retreat of Gen. McClellan in 1862.

This brings to mind personal associations of my own with an esteemed friend whom I first met about the same eventful period, and who subsequently joined us on the march. In '62 we were associated in the army of the Potomac, in '64 in the city of New Orleans, in '65 in St. Louis, and in '66 we journeyed several hundred miles together over the plains of the far West, destined to different and remote posts, possibly to meet again in our army career, possibly only in eternity. We parted warmer friends, after so many accidental, but pleasant, associations. The officer I refer to is Surgeon Alexander, long the popular and efficient Medical Director in the Crescent City.

All things being ready for the march, on the 26th of April, while the weather was yet cool and pleasant, and before the fields were green with the grass of spring, our column may have been seen wending its way over the hills of Kansas in the direction of Ft. Kearney. For several days we did not get beyond the enclosed and cultivated farms, which in the absence of a regularly surveyed public road made our course much more tortuous than when travelling over the unsettled prairie beyond. It seemed at times as if the road passed around three sides of a farm, when there was nothing to interfere with its following the more direct fourth boundary line. But the roads were excellent, and we in no hurry. What difference did it make to us if our 1200 miles journey should be extended five miles by indirect roads?

After passing to the West, and within sight of Atchison, we struck the great overland stage route, along which we marched many hundred miles. The sight of a stage-coach twice daily, and the constant presence of telegraph poles, tended to relieve to some extent those inclined to loneliness. With me it caused frequent thoughts of loved ones far away, with whom such means could speedily communicate, but from whom I must necessarily, for a long time, be separated. From Atchison, Kansas, to California, there is daily a line of stages making the entire journey in sixteen days.* To conduct this great enterprise successfully and profitably, it is necessary that there should be frequent relays of horses, accordingly there are stations all along the line, separated 10 or 12 miles, where the horses are changed, and every 40 or 50 miles is a "Home Station," where the driver changes also, to return over the same road, so that each driver in a short time becomes familiar with every part of his route. At the Home Stations passengers obtain their meals.

The route is divided into Divisions, over each of which is a superintendent; and at the terminus of each Division the passengers, baggage, and mails are transferred to other coaches. All the changes are made expeditiously, and but little delay occurs anywhere. Mr. Benjamin Holladay is the principal proprietor of the stage line, and is a man of remarkable energy and enterprise. I regret that my first favorable impressions of Mr. Holladay and his line did not continue. I will hereafter explain why I do not think him entitled to all the laudations which writers, who have accepted his favors, heap upon him.

Along this part of the route, in addition to the Stage Stations, there are many "Ranches" for the accommodation of emigrants, and also, and more particularly, for the *profit* of the keepers. They are generally constructed of logs and very rudely built, but most of them contain a good assortment of the more essential articles required by

---

*Since the above was written the extension of the Pacific Railroad, westward, along the Platte river, has made Omaha the eastern terminus of the California overland route, instead of Atchison; and passengers already have the monotony of the journey broken by several hundred miles ride in the cars.

A HOME STATION.

the emigrant, as well as some he does not require. Canned fruits and vegetables are conspicuously displayed upon the shelves, making perhaps a greater show for the same cost than other articles the establishment contains, and generally no inconsiderable quantity of "Hostetter's Bitters"—a form in which the emigrant may obtain very poor whiskey at a very high price—occupy prominent places upon the shelves also. In addition to Stations and Ranches there are also several trading towns or villages between Leavenworth and Kearney. Seneca, about six days journey (as we travelled) from Leavenworth, is quite a thriving and enterprising place. I found the cunning Yankee trader at Seneca as well as every where else where a store is kept on the plains, and paid for my dealing with one by being badly cheated in some cigars.

The country over which we passed from Leavenworth to Kearney presents a beautiful, regularly undulating surface, and is watered at convenient distances for daily marches, by numerous streams.

The rolling prairies of Kansas differ widely from the broad plains of Illinois. The reader who has only seen the latter level can form but a poor idea of the beauty and grandure of the former. One who has sailed over the ocean during a calm the day after a storm, and has observed the gentle elevations and depressions of its surface, without a ripple upon the water, and can imagine a vast extent of country, extending far away to the horizon all around, as smooth as the sea, and with the same regular undulations of its surface but magnified a thousand times, can form some idea of the vastness and beauty of the country over which we journeyed from Leavenworth to Kearney.

The atmosphere is clear and rarified, and objects can be seen a long distance. The *mirage* about the horizon adds increasing beauty to the scenery. When observing elevation after elevation far away in the distance, until the last little hill seems to support the cloudy dome, we could see reflected on the sky the appearance of a beautiful silvery lake, with its islands and its trees. To one unaccustomed to the scene, and not informed as to its true nature, the optical delusion is complete. Objects near the horizon with the sky as a back-ground appear of immense size—cows eight or ten miles distant look like elephants, and a David would seem to be more than a Goliath in stature.

This vast uncultivated region is not only pleasing to the eye in viewing its topography, but possesses a fertility of soil unsurpassed, I should suppose, by any farming lands in the country. The slightest cultivation would cause it to yield to the husbandman the most luxurient crops of every product of the richest valleys of New York or Ohio, and we predict for Kansas, when the great highway—the Pacific Railroad—shall have been completed, and emigration poured into the State, an agricultural wealth equal to that of any other part of the Union.

The country as I stated before, is not without water, but many clear and rapidly flowing streams are found in its fertile, and in some instances, cultivated valleys. The names of these streams are not very classic or poetic. We crossed the "Big Sandy," the "Little Sandy," the "Big Blue," "Bull Creek," and the "Big Muddy." But the latter should not be mentioned in the same connection with the prairie streams of this country. It is not a stream at all, except after a rain, but a series of disgusting standing pools which are kept constantly stirred up to almost the consistency of butter-milk, for a mile on either side of the road, by thousands of animals, belonging to the passing trains, being driven into them to drink. Along this part of the route, only, is water scarce; but here for 35 or 40 miles the "Big Muddy" affords the only water, except the small wells at the Stations.

I must tell the reader something of the incidents of our journey, and not confine myself to a description of the country only. Such a trip as ours was certainly an enjoyable one and I enjoyed it in other ways than admiring the scenery. How incomparably more pleasant to travel, as we did, to being rushed over the road, night and day at break-neck speed, in one of Ben Holladay's coaches, be the comforts afforded in the latter all that the ingenuity of the great contractor could offer a Colfax and party.

Our marches were from 18 to 20 miles a day; starting at 5 o'clock in the morning, and going into camp usually about noon. The remainder of the day was spent in such recreations and amusements as the country afforded, and the taste of the indiuidual would lead him to indulge in. But to me the *whole march* was recreation and amusement. Not being required to accompany the column, I wandered off for miles in search of the better game of the country. Everywhere we found birds numerous. For prairie chickens we hunted away from the road: for ducks along the streams, and in the little pones to be found here and there; for the English plover we sought out the marshy places, and there were the snipe also; for the smaller birds—prairie plover, and meadow larks it was not necessary to leave the road, but shoot them from the ambulances as we rode along. Those of us fond of bird-shooting found abundance of such sport, and our tables were daily supplied with at least some luxuries which would be highly relished even in New Orleans where there is always so much to gratify the palate. I remember on one occasion bringing down with the two loads of my gun, nine large English plovers—more than a mess for all the ladies in camp. In the afternoon it was no uncommon thing to catch within a hundred yards of our camp (for we always camped on a stream), a good mess of small pan-fish for our early breakfast the next morning. So with plenty of prairie chickens, ducks, plover, fish, potatoes, and canned vegetables, in variety, there was but little danger of scurvy to be apprehended among those who could indulge in such luxuries.

The evenings were spent in the tents playing chess or cards, or in reading or conversation, according to the inclination of the party. But I early sought the embrace of Morpheus to be willing to rise at the sound of reveille in the morning, which usually was heard at 3½ or 4 o'clock. Think of the trial, in this way imposed upon an individual, who, up to the commencement of the march, indulged in the bad habit of lying in bed in the morning until called to breakfast a 8½ or 9 o'clock, I early adapted myself to the new state of things however, and soon failed to regard it a hardship to rise with the early bird.

No danger was to be apprehended from hostile Indians, south of Fort Kearney, and the only red-skins now in that vicinity are a small band of the Ottoe tribe, who have a settlement on a government reservation a few miles east of the stage road on the Big Blue.

We remained over Sabbath in camp near their village, and many of the officers availed themselves of the opportunity of observing their domestic life, and visited their wigwams, but I was not among the number, preferring to wait until we penetrated further into the Indian country, before studying the habits of the noble (?) Red Man. I saw enough of the Ottoes, however, to satisfy me that they were a set of begging, thieving, filthy, disgusting savages. Though within a short distance of the white settlements they had adopted but few of the customs of the white man which added to their comfort, or advancement in civilization, but had acquired with readiness his vices. They were eager for whiskey, and I observed them gambling at cards with the soldiers when unable to speak a word of English.

They carried away the offal of our slaughtered cattle, and doubtless enjoyed their dinner of it, as one of unusual richness. And this occurred in a country where game is plenty, and the fertile soil yields abundantly of everything cultivated.

Sixteen marches brought us to Fort Kearney. As we approached the place, along the Platte River, it could be distinctly seen when 10 or 12 miles away, and in the mirage, its building loomed up as the tall towers of an ancient castle.

CHAPTER II.

FROM FORT KEARNEY TO FORT MACPHERSON.

WE reached Fort Kearney on the 13th of May. It is one of the oldest posts on the plains, and is situated on the South side of the Platte River, about 200 miles from its mouth. The Platte possesses many of the features of the Missouri, of which it is an important tributary, but is an unnavigable stream, though through its bed flows an immense body of water. It is in places from a mile to a mile and a half in width, and its current as rapid as that of the great stream into which it empties.

The term " Forts," as applied to military posts on the frontier, has caused a very general misconception of their real character. It is the popular opinion, where it has not been corrected, that these forts are works of masonry, or at least extensive earth-works, after the style of our permanent fortifications in the States, or the more elaborate temporary works constructed so extensively in some localities, during the late war. But such is not the case. Fort Kearney, like nearly all the posts I have visited, is without any work of defense—not even a stockade. It consists simply of a number of two story frame buildings, arranged in the usual way around a parade ground, which is the centre of the post, furnishing quarters for the officers and men. There are also additional buildings as store-houses, stables, sutler's stores, &c. There are posts, however, in more dangerous localities, where the quarters are surrounded by a stockade, and others where slight earth-works exist, but such are exceptions to the rule.

Fort Kearney, as I said before is one of the oldest posts on the plains, and the effects of time are plainly visible on the buildings, many of which are quite dilapidated, and some so tottering and frail that huge props extending to the eves are necessary to prevent the high winds, prevailing there, from levelling them to the ground.

In addition to the wooden structures around the parade, there are a number of one-story buildings made of turf. These are not the *adobe* houses of which the reader has doubtless heard, and of which I will give a description at some other time, when we reach a lócality where they are found. The turf houses are structures made by piling fresh sods one upon another in the manner bricks are placed in a wall, with a little soft mud intervening to fill up the interstices. The walls are made from two to three feet thick, and these houses are said to be the most comfortable at the post—warm in winter and cool in summer; but for elegance they will hardly compare with some in the Garden District of New Orleans.

At Kearney we replenished our stock of subsistance stores, and received a large accession to our numbers. Here Col. Carrington, who commands the 18th infantry, was waiting with another battalion for us to join him, and when we did so he commanded the whole. Major Van-Voast, who only temporarily commanded the detachment from Leavenworth, relinquished his position to Brevet Lieut. Col. Lewis, who joined us there, and the former became a guest, as it were, on his way to Fort Laramie, where he now commands. Col. Lewis I found to be in every way worthy to succeed the efficient officer he relieved. It was my good fortune to serve under him, and I shall endeavor at some other time to refer to my appreciation of his abilities as an officer, and his worth as a gentleman and friend. In connection with the other additions to our party, I must not here neglect to mention the ladies. I referred to them last, when mentioning the party that left Leavenworth, and now, again, they are brought in as if not entitled to the first notice. I beg their pardon.

They deserve to be prominent in my memory whenever writing about the command. I was about to say that three additions were made to the little circle of lady associates, and among them Mrs. Carrington, the wife of the Colonel, and the good Mrs. Dr. Horton, whose acquaintance I made in New Orleans nearly two years ago. How delightful to meet friends under such circumstances!

After a halt of a week we cheerfully resumed our journey, every one being weary of the inactive camp-life, and anxious to lessen the distance between us and our destination daily. At Fort Kearney the three principal routes from the East—from Leavenworth, Nebraska City, and Omaha—unite to form the great overland highway for emigrants along the Platte. Here we saw more pilgrims on their westward journey than at any previous time. Emigrants here are universally called "pilgrims," and camping as they do only for a night, and then off again on their journey, makes the term not inappropriate, but to me suggesting loneliness and solitude. Notwithstanding a recent order of Gen. Pope, requiring at least twenty wagons to travel together, and thirty armed men, for defence against the Indians, it was no uncommon thing for two or three wagons only to compose a "train," and in them helpless women and children,

Within the last two or three years many such trains have been attacked and destroyed by the Indians,—the men killed and scalped, and the women made to suffer worse than death, and held as hostages for which large ransoms have been required. To prevent such massacres and outrages, the order forbidding small trains to go into the Indian country was issued. How astonishing it is that emigrants with all the facts before them, should seek to evade an order which contemplates only their own protection; and how especially astonishing, that an emigrant should incur all this risk with a helpless family. But they do it constantly. Trains are organized at the various military posts, but before they have been out two days they divide up into small parties, until they are stopped at the next post, to reorganize.

I was surprised to see so many women among the emigrants, and to see how easily they adapted themselves to the hardships required in a journey across the plains. As a rule they travel without tents, sleep in and under their wagons without removing their clothes, cook their bacon and flour in a frying pan, or sometimes in a dutch oven over a fire of "buffalo chips;" but they seem to enjoy vigorous health, and appear contented and happy. One of the best drivers of a four horse wagon I observed on the plains was a woman.

In addition to the trains going West, we met quite a number belonging to freighters travelling in an opposite direction. They had wintered beyond the mountains, and were now making their usual summer trip. To curtail drivers as well as rest the oxen, several wagons, for they were empty, were tied one behind the other, and the oxen of the first drew them all, while those thus rendered supernumary were driven in herds along with the train.

Throughout our march, but particularly along this part of the route, where the travel is so extensive, the road is strewn with the remains of animals who have perished by the way. From the recently dead beast, to the whitened bones of those that had died long ago, their remains could be seen almost constantly. Interspersed with the bones of the cattle were numerous buffalo skulls, unmistakeable traces of the buffalo hunter in times past. These skulls and the old buffalo-trails made when they sought the Platte for water, or to cross in their yearly northern migration, were the only indications we had that the animal ever frequented the valley. At one time the buffalo were as numerous in this section of the country as anywhere on the plains. I was informed by an officer who was stationed at Fort Kearney, in 1853 that they were so numerous in that vicinity during the summer of that year, as to require on one occasion a piece of artillery to drive large herds from the immediate vicinity of the fort, as there was danger of them being stampeded and rushing through the post, endangering life and property. The old order book of that time is still at the Fort, and corroborates the statement of the officer.

The only wild quadruped game now to be found in the vicinity is the antelope. Their fleetness and timidity, however, prevented us from securing any there,but subsequently, along another part of our journey, quite a number were shot, as I shall hereafter mention.

The country in the valley of the Platte bore an entirely different aspect from that lying South of it, which we have already described. Here the surface was as level as around New-Orleans, and as far as the eye could reach up and down the river not the least irregularity could be observed between the Bluffs on the South, and the river on the North. It is to that portion of the valley contiguous to Kearney, that I refer; further West it assumes a somewhat undulating surface. Though different in appearance from the country I admired so much, and referred to in my first letter, this possessed a beauty of scenery in comparison not to be despised. The Platte river is filled with islands,ranging in size from a half acre,or less of surface,to one 60 miles long; and upon them are trees, and many of the smaller ones are covered with an undergrowth of shrubbery, while on the main land not a bush or a tree is to be seen. But here the prairie grass was just assuming its richest green, and the lovely little wild prairie-flowers represented vegetation in a form quite as attractive as on the verdant islands. In places, the beautiful purple and white blossoms covered the ground so thickly as to almost hide the young grass; and here and there grew the cactus.

To the South lay the sand buttes,as they are called,which increased in heighth, and became more abrupt as we proceeded Westward. These and similar ones far away on the North of the river where doubtless the banks of an immense stream which covered this whole valley not many centuries ago. From the highest of these buttes a magnificent view of the valley and river could be had, and I availed myself of the opportunity of seeing the country from one of them. I found a few friends to accompany me, and arming with carbines and pistols (for this had been a favorite locality for Indian depredations the year before) we started for the hills, which looked to be about a mile away; but the distance on the plains is very deceptive, and it required a ride of three or four miles before we reached their summit. The ascent, as we approached, looked so gentle as to permit of riding up at a canter, but we found it so steep upon approaching nearer, as to render it difficult even to lead our animals to the top; but we reached it, and remained for an hour in admiration of the magnificent view which was there afforded. For twenty miles either way the broad surface of the Platte, dotted with its islands of verdure, could be seen in all its windings; and, between it and the range of hills, the broad valley covered with the new prairie grass in all its richness. Far away on the banks of the stream were the white tents of our camp, which looked like a bed of mushrooms, and the herd of animals grazing nearer to the foot of the hills appeared like a pack of hunter's hounds. South of us was a succession of hills and ravines—the former of sand and without vegetation; the latter covered with long grass looking greener because of the contrast with the barren hills surrounding them. The sight was altogether one of the grandest I had then ever beheld, but I subsequently found that it was only initiative to greater grandeur and beauty which awaited me in the mountains further west. The sand buttes of the Platte were as the Rocky Mountains in miniature.

Along this valley, only a year ago, the Indians had perpetrated the most barbarous murders, as well as destroyed a large amount of property. The country is a peculiarly adapted for their depredations. The hills in some places are but little removed from the river, affording the savages a most excellent place for concealment. From these hills they watched for trains incapable of resisting on attack, and sallied forth upon the defenceless emigrant, with whom retreat was impossible because of the river on the other side, and he fell an easy victim to his brutal foe.

Not only were trains attacked, ranches pillaged and destroyed, but the occupants murdered. In many instances the latter abandoned their property, and sought safety at the military posts. We passed the ruins of a large ranche where $20,000 worth of goods had been destroyed last July, the owner having left the premises only a day or two before the savages were upon them. At Plum Creek, our second camp from Kearny, were a large number of graves of settlers who were murdered and scalped at the time I referred to. All along the road graves of emigrants were seen daily, generally solitary, but sometimes three or four together, and almost invariably we found inscribed upon a rough head-board the name of the individual buried there, and "killed by the Indians July—, 1865."

I will defer any comments upon these barbarities for a future letter, in which I propose to write more about the Indians of the plains than space would allow to be included in this. Notwithstanding the destruction of life and property along the Platte within so recent a period, the ranches are as numerous this season, if not more numerous than before. The great incentive men have for conducting these establishments is the profit arising from their sales, and when we consider the risk incurred, and the discomforts to which the keepers are subjected, the large profits asked on the goods seemed not so unreasonable after all.

Most of the ranches, in dangerous localities are constructed with a view to defence against the Indians. The houses and stables have loop holes from which the occupants may fire upon an attacking party, and in some large corrals for the cattle surrounded by a wall of sods connected with the ranches, afforded a still further protection against the treacherous enemies of the white man.

In this locality nearly all the ranches are built of turf, like the buildings at Fort Kearney, which I have described. In many instances the roofs are of the same material, and constructed by placing thatch upon a few timbers and upon this is laid the sods. Such roofs in Louisiana, during the wet season, would not be considered very desirable, but out here where but little rain falls they answer the purpose very well. The scarcity of timber, and the high price it commands, prevents it from entering into the construction of ranches excep to a very limited extent, and generally not even for floors.

Six marches from Kearney took us to Cottonwood Springs, where Fort McPherson is located. We reached that point on the 24th of May.

CHAPTER III.

FROM FORT MCPHERSON TO FORT SEDGWICK.

Fort McPherson, so called after the able and gallant general who was killed in Georgia in 1864, was built about the time of the death of the distinguished officer whose name it bears. It presents a neat compact appearance, and is one of the few military posts surrounded by a stockade. Its buildings are one-story log structures, rather rustic in appearance, but I considered it as altogether a more desirable post than its next easterly and more venerable neighbor, Fort Kearney.

Fort McPherson is located on a small stream running into the Platte, familiar to the western traveller as Cotton Wood Springs. It is about one hundred miles distant from Fort Kearney, and is regarded as a post of considerable military importance, being in a country where frequent Indian depredations have been committed. There were six companies, four of Infantry, and two of Cavalry garrisoning the post when we passed.

Having no business there, the command marched by without even a halt, rather to the disappointment of the sutler, I have no doubt.

While on this day's march, in the vicinity of the Fort, we lost one of our number—a citizen employed as clerk for the Quartermaster, which was the only death that occurred during our three months' journey, save several from an accident to which I shall hereafter refer. We buried the poor man at our next camping ground, and the plain cedar head-board of his grave now stands, another sad spectacle to the passing emigrant. His wife and several children continued a mournful journey along with us to Salt Lake City, whither the husband and father was going to reside.

The Platte river is formed by the confluence of two streams—the North and South Platte, which takes place a few miles west of the mouth of Cottonwood. Our journey then lay along the South Platte. Some change in character of the country and scenery, was to be observed. The disappearance of the range of hills on the south, and the valley merging into the broad prairie, gave it rather a different aspect. About ten miles west of Fort McPherson is Jack Morrow's Ranche, one of the largest on the plains.

It was the latter part of May when we journeyed along the Platte. The new grass which had not appeared on the prairies of Kansas, had here sufficiently matured to afford excellent pasturage for our animals. It was desirable that the column should make an early start, and it moved from Leavenworth before there was grass on the prairies for the mules. They had been fed on hay, purchased at the ranches along the route, and in some instances at enormously high prices; but here there was no need of hay, and as soon as the train was parked, the mules were all turned out to graze. This was my first march with a mule-train, and I observed much in the habits of that animal that surprised me. In the first place, I was surprised to see how easily a large herd of them can be controlled. Three or four herders would have no difficulty in keeping together as many hundred mules. They were allowed to graze only during the day, and at night when they were to be tied up to their wagons, they were brought in without the least difficulty. The wagon-master would take out a little grey horse, fasten a bell to his neck, and start from the herd towards camp, when every mule would stop grazing, and follow on. As they approached the wagons, each would select his own and go to it, to be haltered and fed for the night. After observing this and other things in their habits, I came to the conclusion that the mule is a much slandered animal, and will never refer to him again as an example of stupidity. He fully bore out his reputation for obstinacy, however.

Ranches continued as numerous along the Platte as they were south of Kearney. In referring to these establishments in my first letter, I neglected to mention a very important item in their business, viz., the sale of grain and hay to emigrants, during the season when animals cannot subsist on the grass. The grain is brought from the Missouri river, and commands a very high price, but the hay is the wild grass that grows on the prairie, which is cut in the summer, and stacked up until there is a demand for it.

The most extensive ranch or trading post I have seen on the plains is one conducted by a Frenchman named Beauvais. It is on the South Platte where the old California road crosses that stream, and is known as the "California Crossing." Beauvais has accumulated a large fortune since he started this ranch. His principal profits are from his advantageous trading with the Indians. This he does on a very large scale, and it is the common talk on the plains that the savages obtain from him arms and ammunition with which emigrants are murdered, in exchange for robes and skins. He may be innocent of the charge, but it is a singular fact that the Indians have never disturbed Monsieur Beauvais' establishment, when almost every other ranch in that part of the country has been destroyed, at some time, and there has always been more plunder to be had at the California Crossing than at any of the ranches destroyed.

Agricultural pursuits are entirely neglected by the settlers in the Platte Valley, though the soil and climate are such in my opinion, as would produce the cereals if not more delicate vegetable growths. In almost every respect it has the advantage of New England as an agricultural country. The great draw-backs are the dryness of the summer months, and the high winds that prevail. The former could be overcome by irrigation as in Salt Lake Valley. After seeing what has been accomplished there by this means I shall not hereafter consider the absence of rain as a serious objection to a country where irrigation can be resorted to. No difficulty would attend its adoption along the Platte, and then the moisture necessary for vegetable life would be more certainly afforded than is done by the rains in the most favored agricultural districts.

The absence of timber is another draw-back. Not a tree grows upon the banks of the Platte, and those on the islands are entirely inadequate to the demand that would arise for wood in a settled country. In the vicinity of Cotton Wood Springs some cedar and cotton wood grow, back in the bluffs, but with this exception the entire country from Kearney to Sedgwick is entirely without timber.

Before starting from Leavenworth I provided myself with a mosquito bar as an important article in my out-fit, and in making up another for a similar trip I shall be as careful to add a ladies' tissue veil. Mosquitoes are very annoying insects; but I think the little buffalo gnats are, I was going to say infinitely more so. To keep them off the face and neck is what the veil would be used for. During two or three marches along the Platte after a rain, these gnats proved exceedingly annoying. They are so small, that their presence on the skin is not detected until the irritation of their bite makes it known. Their favorite locality seemed to be on the neck and behind the ears, and so thick would they collect, that after their bite not a particle of the skin of these parts would be free from the swelling and inflammation.

While on the march from McPherson to Sedgwick one of the officers of our battallion very narrowly escaped death at the hands of a soldier belonging to another command. The man had straggled, and was indulging rather freely in Hostetter's Bitters in a ranch by the roadside, when the rear-guard came up, and he was ordered by the officer in command to go forward. Some hesitation and insubordination occurred on the part of the soldier, when he was struck with the side of the officer's sword. He then rode forward, borrowed a musket (as he was unarmed) "to shoot an antelope" as he represented, loaded it and fell back again. When opposite our command he thought he recognized Lieutenant Gill as the man who struck him, and going up to that officer accused him of doing so, at the same time cocking his musket, with the muzzle within three feet of the breast of the officer, he pulled the trigger and exploded the cap; but fortunately did not discharge the piece. The man was immediately arrested, and his musket examined, which was found to be loaded, and the explosion of another cap sent the ball into the ground. The scoundrel was put in irons to be tried by a Court-Martial, at the next post, but managed to make his escape the following night.

A march of one hundred miles brought us to Julesburg, a place destined to be of much importance as a trading post, though at present it consists of not over a half dozen houses of all kinds. In 1864, the first settlement by this name was entirely destroyed by the Indians, and with it a considerable quantity of stores, including a large stock of grain belonging to the overland stage company. But the settlers have not been discouraged, and are now rebuilding the city(?), with apparently no apprehensions of a repetition of Indian outrages. Their houses are of a more substantial character, and are constructed at a greater expense than any others on the plains. Most of them are built of lumber brought from Denver, a distance of 200 miles, though there are some of the Mexican *adobe* structure. This is a spanish word, and on the plains is unusually pronounced as if spelled *doby*. The adobe brick consists of a mixture of clay and sand, moulded in a way, and of a shape similar to our brick in the East, but of a larger size, and are dried in the sun only. It answers well as a substitute for the ordinary building brick when it is impracticable to obtain te latter. A soft mud of the same material is used as mortar, and a house so constructed with its walls smoothly plastered over makes both a neat and comfortable residence in a dry climate.

Near Julesburg the great overland emigrant route divides. One branch of it crosses the river, and going by way of Fort Laramie, through the South Pass of the Rocky Mountains, continues on to the Pacific; while the other follows the South Platte to Denver, and thence by a northerly course enters Bridger's Pass, and unites again with the former about 40 miles east of Fort Bridger. The Denver route is the one taken by the overland mail coaches.

Where this division occurs, Fort Sedgwick is located. This is considered as a post of even more importance than Fort McPherson, and has been more recently established. After the destruction of Julesburg by the Indians in '64, the Government sent troops to this point for greater security to emigration, as well as for the protection of the mail route. These troops erected temporary quarters for the winter on a site, not selected with a view to its permanency as a military post.

But as Boston was built along its cow-paths for convenience, so these temporary quarters were added to and enlarged, and finally the new garrison of Fort Sedgwick is being built there. The officer who first camped on this spot, probably had no more idea of its being the nucleus of a large and important post, than had the early settlers along the cow-paths of that locality becoming the "Hub of the Universe." Fort Sedgwick is built upon a slightly elevated piece of land, and will present a very pretty appearance, after the completion of the quarters, and the removal of several unsightly structures which can then be dispensed with. This is one of the most expensive military stations on the plains. For example, the Government paid for all the wood used there last winter, (and soldiers and officers used their full allowance, for it is a cold and bleak situation), *one hundred and fourteen dollars* a cord; and a necessity occurred for the Commissary to buy potatoes on the spot, for which he paid about $9 a bushel.

Here we made our next halt for a few days, and enjoyed much a short respite from daily marches. Contemplating this halt, the soldiers had made preparation for quite a novel exhibition in such a locality, and under such circumstances. A number of good singers and mimics had been practising for several days as Ethopian minstrels, and with the permission of the commanding officer gave a grand concert on the second night in camp. They were allowed the use of two large hospital tents, and every facility afforded them for making their entertainment as successful as possible. Nearly all the officers in our command, as well as those at the garrison with their families attended the performance, which I was told (for I was not present) was exceedingly creditab e, and conducted with more propriety than sometimes attend similar demonstrations in our large cities. Such performances are now becoming quite popular at many posts on the frontier.

Here we parted with the first detachment that left our command. Two companies left for Fort Wardwell, which is located near Denver, one remained at Fort Sedgwick, and the remainder crossed the river for stations further north and west.

The melting of snow in the mountains causes the streams to be much swollen at this season, and apprehensions had been felt by the Col. of the regiment that he would be unable to ford the river with his command. Accordingly he had taken the precaution, before leaving Kearney, to order the construction of a large ferry-boat, which was completed when we arrived; but the ferry was yet an experiment, and proved to be as unsuccessful as was Robinson Crusoe's first effort at navigation. The boat was launched, however, without difficulty; but when it got into the water it proved to be entirely too large to be managed in the swift current, and too heavy to float in the shallow water on the bars in the stream. The ferry, therefore, was a failure, and was abandoned.

There we were, with a wide and rapid stream in front of us—formidable looking, and too deep, it was supposed, to be forded. Various conjectures were made, as to what should be done, when Major Norris of the 2d Cavalry came up with two companies of his regiment to cross the river also, he being en route for Fort Laramie. The Major has been marching over the plains, and crossing streams for about half his life, and is not to be discouraged by trifles. He was familiar with the Platte, and as soon as he came up said it was fordable. Col. Carrington disagreed with the Major, but as he was not under the Col's command, he insisted on attempting to cross his train. Giving "Pigeon" (his favorite horse) to his First Sergeant, the Major directed him to go into the river and find the best fording place, which was done immediately, when the wagons followed, and then the men. Profiting by the example, the next day the Infantry and their train crossed also without accident or the loss of a dollar's worth of property, public or private. The rapid stream proved to be only a bug-bear; and the Major by his bold example, saved us an additional march of 200 miles, by way of Denver, which was seriously talked about when he arrived.

It was cold weather for fording streams. Early the following morning the thermometer indicated 33°, and two days thereafter I had equally reliable evidence of a still lower temperature. Upon rising on the 6th of June I found ice an eighth of an inch thick on the water in a bowl in my tent awaiting my morning ablution. Our marches still commenced at an early hour, and about this time I often found it necessary for comfort to abandon my horse and walk briskly for an hour or two with my overcoat on. And this occurred in a latitude less than a degree North of that of St. Louis, and at no great elevation. I often thought when shivering with cold, of my sensations in New Orleans at the same season and at the same hour of the morning when the sea breeze had not sprung up to make the heat tolerable, and I concluded that I would rather shiver in the pure, dry, cold, invigorating atmosphere of the Northwest, than sweat and swelter in the hot, humid enervating climate of the beautiful Crescent City in the month of June.

Safely across the river the entire command commenced its westward march along Lodge Pole Creek, and two days thereafter more than half the column destined to Fort Laramie and posts North of it separated.

The night before this occurred all the officers, who were to continue the westward route, collected at the quarters of Col. Carrington to take leave of him and his estimable lady. Sad memories are connected with that little assemblage. Capt. Brown, who was then quartermaster of one of the batallions was the most jovial, and best contented man as to his destination in the company. He cracked jokes about being scalped, and seemed to fear such a fate less than any one present; but alas! he was first to fall by the hands of the Indian he so little feared. He was one of the victims of the horrid massacre near Fort Phil Kearny last December.

Our company of ladies was reduced proportionately with the command. Three left us at Sedgwick, three more on the occasion just alluded to, and three continued on towards the City of the Saints.

CHAPTER IV.

ALONG LODGE POLE CREEK.

Lodge Pole Creek is a stream rising in the "Black Hills" and running in an easterly direction to the South Platte, into which it empties, in the vicinity of Julesburg. Near its source is an extensive growth of straight, slender trees, which are used by the Indians in the construction of the lodges; hence the name of the creek.

An Indian Lodge consists of a conical frame-work of

small poles tied together at the apex, over which is placed a covering of tanned skins, sewed together in a shape and of a size to make a smooth surface. A lodge so constructed has the appearance of Sibley tents, with the ends of the poles projecting from the top. The tent I refer to is constructed upon a precisely similar principle, but with a centre pole as a substitute for those used in the lodges. The Indian builds his fire in the centre of his lodge, and the smoke escapes through the top, while the tents have the improvement of a stove, generally, though I have seen fires built in them as in Indian lodges.

To the Aborigines, then, we are indebted for the principle upon which one of our most extensively used tents is made.

The course of Lodge Pole Creek is through a valley, the sides of which gently ascend to the level of the extended prairie, both North and South. The valley abounds in rich nutritious grass, and has a soil, which at some period, will doubtless yield abundantly of many of the staple agricultural products of our country. This valley is the natural route for the Pacific Railroad, after leaving South Platte River; but whether or not local influence will prevail, and take it over some other, time only will determine. The expense attending its construction here would be very trifling compared with that of building it by the way of Denver, but the influence of Colorado will probably take it to that city.* Should it fail, then another Denver, more prosperous than the present, will spring up as by magic at some point in this valley.

Lodge Pole Creek possesses many peculiarities, and not least among them is its entire disappearance, for miles, in some places. This strange phenomenon is not owing to a

---

*Since this was written the commissioners of the Pacific Railroad have determined that the road shall be built along Lodge Pole Creee, and enter the Black Hills at a pass about 20 miles south of Cheyenne Pass, down which the creek flows. As the road can be constructed along this valley as rapidly as it has been along the Platte the probability is that it will be completed throngh the Black Hills by the spring or summer of 1868.

subterranean passage, but is accounted for in the character of the soil which forms the bed of the stream. Where this disappearance takes plaee, it is of a coarse sand extending to a considerable depth, and as the water enters the sandy soil it sinks below the surface, and percolates through it until the character of the bed changes again, when the stream appears on the surface as before. Where it is hidden there is generally a dry sandy place above it, and by digging into this a foot below the surface the water can be seen pursuing its course towards the visible stream below. The course of the occasional disappearance of the creek operates also in producing great variation in its size. At one place it may be seen a narrow, sluggish stream, and a mile or two above, when passing over a bed of clay, it assumes a large size with a brisk current. I said this occasional disappearance of the stream was a peculiarity of Lodge Pole Creek; but I have been informed that such is a characteristic of the majority of the streams west of the Rocky Mountains. It was a novelty to me, and I have not visited the country where this is common. Along this creek, which "for short" is called "Pole Creek," I saw for the first time the ingeniously constructed beaver dams. In the abscence of large timber they are made of twigs placed vertically, with one end imbedded in the bottom of the stream, and other twigs placed transwisely, and against the sort of net work thus formed, a thick layer of earth is piled so as to offer a sufficient resistance to the greatest pressure of water that a rise in the stream may bring against it. Above the dams they construct their houses. Some are built up from the bottom of the stream, in the middle of it, and rounded off like a dome just above the surface of the water; but here they are made, principally, by burrowing into the banks with the dome-like top on the main land, instead of forming an island. The entrance to both classes are under water. The Beaver is exceedingly shy, and while I have seen hundreds of dams and houses, and hundreds more of their skins after they have been dressed by the Indians, I have not yet seen one of the animals.

The antelope, which appeared only occasionally along the Platte, were here to be seen in great numbers, bounding over the hills as the column marched along. They were very timid, however, and to hunt them successfully, required a greater degree of labor and patience than I was disposed to bestow upon the sport. The more experienced hunters among the soldiers, however, secured a large number of them in this valley and on the hills bordering it. We found a roast of tender antelope meat not an undesireable substitute for beef occasionally, and I relished very much this, to me, new diet.

The antelope is a neat, gracefully formed animal, resembling much the deer, with perhaps shorter legs. It is about the size of a deer, with short branched horns; is of a light brown or yellowish brown color on the back, white under the belly and has short, white, rather bushy tails. I alluded to them as *bounding* over the hills, I might almost with propriety called it *gliding*. They have not a long and high bound like the deer, but leap close to the ground, and at a distance appear to glide along with but little exertion; their motions are so regular and gentle. that a very imperfect idea of their fleetness is formed when not compared with the speed of other animals.

They are animals of remarkable curiosity, and this is taken advantage of in hunting them. A small red flag will decoy them to a spot where the hunter lies ready to shoot, and secure his game. A passing wagon will attract their attention; and even when hotly pursued, they will yield to the promptings of their curiosity, and stop occasionally, turn around, raise their heads and very deliberately gaze at their pursuer for a moment, and then dash off again. They get demoralized, as the soldiers say, sometimes, and run right into danger. On one occasion I saw an antelope run by the entire column within fifty yards, and at least twenty-five shots were fired at him without effect. They are exceedingly difficult to shoot when in motion.

I well remember my first exciting race after one of them. I thought I had a chance to head him off so as to get within pistol range; so away I dashed, my horse participating in the excitement, and running with a swiftness that astonished me; but I soon saw how useless it was, for the antelope was travelling at the rate of two miles to my one. They are killed in large number by the Indians, and their meat dried for food, while their skins are tanned and dressed, and traded like the deer (buck) skin, but are not considered so valuable. Quite a number of young antelopes were caught by the soldiers, and taken along by the ladies as pets; but they all died or were abandoned because of the difficulty in carrying them, and the scarcity of milk upon which they require to be fed. The antelope zoologically considered, ranges between a goat and a deer. They are much more gracefully formed than the former, and while they are quite as pretty as the latter, they are fleeter animals.

Along Lodge Pole Creek, as elsewhere on the plains, the little prairie dog abounds. This animal has really no resemblance to a dog, but having a sharp bark like one is called so in consequence. Its shape is more like a squirrel, and it belongs to that family. It has not the long tail, however, and their average size is about twice that of the little animal it resembles. They are by no means solitary in their habits, but hundreds of them are found together in their "towns." They bore into the ground, and throw the loose earth into little round piles beside the holes. A large number of these holes, near together, constitute a prairie-dog town or village, as it is called. Some of them are spread out over many acres of ground. They have the reputation of selecting strange bed-fellows, and it it is said an owl, a snake, and a prairie-dog will occupy the same hole. I cannot vouch for the truthfulness of this from personal observation.

On one occasion I came nearly shooting myself, and did shoot my horse, while attempting to fire at an impudent little fellow who sat on the pile of dirt by his hole, not five rods away, barking as the soldiers marched by. Not being able to make my horse stand until I could get a good aim,

I started to dismount, determined to have a shot, and when in the act of doing so, the pistol was accidentally discharged, the ball taking effect in the neck of the horse, and he staggered for a while as if fatally wounded. My own head was so near the pistol at the time, that for a moment or two I could not realize whether I was shot and reeling, or the horse under me.

The rattlesnake was also found along this as well as other parts of the route. As they lay sunning themselves in the road, the men several times came near treading upon them; but when he made known his presence by sounding his rattle, he was given a pretty wide berth until despatched. This was always attended to as faithfully as if the soldier regarded it as a sacred duty. One man would mash his head with the butt of his gun, and another would immediately grab the rattles from his tail. This was my first experience with his snakeship, and I haven't the slightest affinity for him. The noise made by a species of grasshopper is so similar, that I have more than once been startled by it, thinking it was a snake.

This part of our journey was lonesome enough, though the route is much more direct to Utah and beyond; the emigrants avoid it because of the danger of being attacked by Indians; the mail coaches pass south of it by way of Denver; and not even our old companions, the telegraph posts are to be found here—they go north to Laramie. From the Platte to a point near the Big Laramie River, where we again struck the stage line, a solitary train was all we saw to break the monotony of our daily marches; and, save the drivers of this train, not a human face was seen, except those of our own command, in a journey of ten days and nearly 200 miles. The train belonged to the sutler at Fort Bridger, and was on the way to the river to bring out goods. Two of the ladies were to stop at the post it was from, and many were the inquiries made concerning the quarters at the post, and various other matters that they considered would be conducive to their comfort there. We passed the remains of a train burnt by the Indians last fall, and the graves of several who had fallen by the same hands at different periods.

Along this route, and indeed throughout the valleys and flat lands extending from the main Platte to the Pacific coast, there are deposits of an alkaline substance (a salt of soda) to be found on the surface of the ground. I learn, from reliable authority, that in places on the northern route it is found to the depth of a foot; but where we travelled it formed only a small coating over the ground where it had been dissolved by the rain, and deposited again upon the surface in a white powder, after the evaporation of the water.

On the 7th of June we encountered one of those terrific hail storms, so common on the plains. Early in the evening a cloud was observed just above the western horizon. It attracted but little attention at first, as the wind was blowing directly towards it, and we supposed the storm would not reach us, but an upper current caused the cloud to approach rapidly. The eastern wind soon changed to one from the opposite direction, and between eight and nine o'clock it blew with the violence of a tornado, and with it came a few drops of rain. Immediately afterwards the hail commenced; at first only a few pieces of moderate size mixed with the rain, but in a short time the whole of the cloud seemed to have congealed, and fell in fragments as large as black walnuts, and with a velocity and force that was terrific, and in a few minutes almost covered the ground. The night was intensely dark, and during the frightful storm the flashes of lightning followed each other in quick succession, and with painful brilliancy; and the roar of the thunder together with the noise of the hail stones striking the tent-poles, sounded like artillery in battle amidst the rattle of musketry.

I felt confident that our new stout canvass tents would be perforated, and that the mules would break from their fastenings and stampede; and feared serious personal injury to any who might be exposed; but much to my surprise and gratification, I learned, when it was over, that no accident whatever had occurred. So thick was the hail that large quantities of it lay on the ground until sunrise the next morning.

CHAPTER V.

THROUGH THE BLACK HILLS.

As we marched westward along Lodge Pole Creek the Black Hills in which the stream rises came in view; but at the same time appeared a grander sight, the snow-clad summits of the Medicine Bow Mountains looming up conspicuously away to the southwest. They were the first mountains covered with perennial snow that I had seen, and after gazing at them for a long time I began to doubt their reality, thinking it possible in this country of strange freaks of nature a white cloud hanging about the horizon might assume the appearance of the object before me. But another day's march, and a clearer atmosphere, made the outlines of Long's Peak, which has an elevation of 14,000 feet above the sea, as well as the summit of the adjacent range so distinct that no question could then arise as to their true character. All doubts being settled as to what we saw, the officers then commenced estimating the distance that separated the mountains from us, and their estimates varied from 30 to 60 miles; but a two days' journey somewhat in their direction when they were still apparently as far away as when first observed, as well as a reference to my map, told me to conclude that the highest estimate should have been increased at least one half to get the real distance.

On most of the popular maps, this spur of the Rocky Mountains is styled the Meridian Ridge, or the Meridian Bow Ridge, but on the topographical charts of the army, it is put down as I have written it, and is so called by the mountaineers who are familiar with the country. Why it is designated Medicine Bow I have not learned.

The flowers of the Prairie were here quite different in variety from those before observed, but not the less beautiful. The cactus which is found almost everywhere on the plains and mountains, assumes a different form with the changes in the character of the soil in which it grows. Instead of the flat oblong leaf with which we had previously met the oval shaped prickly-pear was to be found abundant here; and at this season their crimson and yellow blossoms were just opening in all their freshness and beauty. For richness of color I think they were unsurpassed by any flowers that I had ever seen. How enjoyable to a class in botany would be a summer's trip over the plains of Nebraska and Colorado!

Reaching the Black Hills—probably so called from the black appearance the growth of cedar on them presents, we encamped for the night in the mouth of a beautiful canon, the former site of a military post known as Fort Walbach. *Canon* pronounced kanyon, is a Spanish word, meaning a valley or a pass in the mountains, and is universally used throughout the far West. I think I never heard a frontiersman use the word valley. I remember an anecdote told of the old mountaineer, James Bridger; how he made rather an odd use of his frontier nomenclature. He is said to have visited St. Louis, and stopped at the Planters' House. After registering his name he looked out, and observed a crowd of people passing down Third Street as is usual during business hours, and turning to the clerk inquired, "what in——was going on down the *Canon* to attract so many people."

Our camping ground at Fort Walbach was a very picturesque one and appeared the more beautiful after marching through a country of so much sameness of scenery, and of so different a character. On either side of us were the smooth but somewhat abrupt slopes of immense hills, and the valley between, thickly covered with tall grass, was watered by a clear mountain stream running through it;

and from the side of the hill gushed out a large spring of delicious water of a temperature requiring no ice to cool it.

The next morning we commenced the hilly part of our journey, and these hills, like the whole mountainous region beyond, possess much interest to the geologist. We crossed the range in one day's march, the entire road being of ascents and descents until we passed over into Laramie Plain on the West. In one of the depressions where the road was bad, and the column was halted to assist in getting the wagons along, I found the trees covered with the names of travellers who had probably stopped for a similar purpose. A foolish way of seeking fame, if to such the parties who inscribed their names there aspired! Along the eastern slope of the highest of these hills, and by the way I can't understand why they are not called a mountain range. The definition of hills and mountains as given in the geographies of my school-boy days left the scholar to make a very capricious distinction between them, and what I might, upon their authority, after a journey over the plains, call a mountain, an old hunter fresh from Long's Peak or Fremont's might upon the same authority call a hill. But I was about to write, when I digressed, that upon these eminences, banks of snow were still remaining when we crossed in the middle of June. Making snow-balls at that season was rather a novel employment for me.

When we reached the summit of the most westerly of the range, there opened out before us the grandest landscape view of my life. Without any knowledge of that topography of the country I was approaching, I rode leisurely ahead of the column, and upon ascending to the brow of a hill, as suddenly as a panoramic painting is brought to the view after the withdrawal of the curtain, so suddenly appeared this natural panorama, more sublime than was ever depicted upon canvass. My pen is inadequate to a just description of its grandeur and beauty, and I can convey to the reader but a faint idea of the scene that then lay before me. I doubt if the editor of the ADVOCATE when he crossed the renowned Alps a few years ago witnessed a sight more grand and magnificent. Far away to the South and Southeast were the snow-clad mountains that attracted our attention for days before reaching the Black Hills. Their tallest peaks only were visible to us then, but now I beheld the whole majestic range with summits as white with snow as in January, and shining under the rays of a noon-day sun in the month of June. The Black Hills upon which I stood extended from a point not far removed from the mountains to which I have just referred, in a northerly, and then changing their course to a westerly direction, making with the mountains a somewhat irregular triangular shape. Long distances separated the two ranges, it is true, but these spaces were not to be seen from where I stood, and the mountains appear to completely surround a basin which is the wide extended Laramie Plain. From my standpoint the ground below appeared to be as level as an Illinois prairie, and for many miles could be seen the road over which we were to travel, looking like a narrow Indian trail through the green prairie grass. The Big Laramie River rising in the Medicine Bow Mountains was ever winding through the plain in its course towards the North Platte; and far beyond the Black Hills to the northeast loomed up the solitary but lofty Laramie Peak. Look which way I might, the grandest prospect met my gaze; but that part of the scene which most absorbed my attention was the elevated glistening summits of the snowy mountains to the south. What a sight for a landscape painter!

The view had its inspiring effect upon the soldiers as well as upon myself. Marching in the hot sun up a long hill had caused a perfect silence in the ranks, which may always be noticed when the men are fatigued, but as they reached the brow of the hill, and beheld what I have endeavored to describe they seemed to be invigorated with new life, and the loud hum of conversation extended along the whole column. It was not a scene to inspire enthusiasm, but profound and subdued wonder and admiration.

Not until I started to descend did I realize the elevation

from which I had this extended view. The road to the base of the hill (but I must now call it a mountain) looked to be about a mile long, but an hour's ride did not take me beyond the slope. When upon this plain I could not recognize it as the one I had seen from the eminence, for instead of its proving to be level, as it appeared, I found an undulating surface like the rolling prairies of Kansas on a smaller scale.

Reaching the river where we were to encamp, after a long and weary ride I lay upon the grass still reviewing the mountain scenery and watching the little silvery clouds assume fantastic shapes upon the clear blue sky, and wondering, admiring and worshipping I fell asleep upon my grassy couch.

Immediately after going into camp, we were visited by a small war party of the Sioux Indians, who were anything but belligerently inclined when they saw the number of men we had. A war party may be known by the absence of squaws, and of lodges, and by all the men being mounted. True to the Indian character, our visitors became beggars, but did not succeed in getting any rations or anything else, and soon left rather disgusted with their reception. Fearing that they would be still further true to the Indian character, an extra guard was placed over the mules that night; but they made no attempt to steal, and probably left the vicinity at once.

The next morning the soldiers indulged in an early cold bath in fording the Big Laramie which was high from the melting snow in the mountains, and the water waist deep; but the men had become accustomed to such performances and waded in as cheerfully as if taking a morning bath at Cape May in the month of August. But to me the sight of others in such cold water on such a cold morning was almost a shock to my nervous system!

Our wagon-master, who had been over this country several times before, had raised my expectations in regard to hunting. When travelling along the Platte River and Lodge Pole Creek, looking in vain for a bird to shoot, he would tell me to be patient until we reached the Black Hills and Laramie Plain, where sage hares and jackass rabbits he represented would be almost innumerable. But all my anticipations were doomed to disappointment, as not a rabbit or a grouse was seen. It may have been the country for them, but it certainly was not the season in that country. Here the sage brush upon which the birds feed began to appear, and afterwards we passed over almost interminable fields of it.

In the Medicine Bow Mountains, in this vicinity, Elk were reported as very numerous, and I presume they must have been, from the fact that elk meat was sold in this country of exorbitant prices at a few cents per pound, and less than the government paid for beef at the next post. There on our journey for the first time, I indulged in a roast of elk meat for my dinner. It had been hanging in the dry, rarified air of that elevated region, until it was near that condition when it could hang no longer, and had become as tender as a spring chicken and as delicious too.

I do not pretend to be a *connoisseur* of meats, but I can't understand in what condition the gustatory organs of writers could have been, when they refer to elk meat as coarse, dry and unpalatable. My cook was not specially skilful in his art, nor had I been deprived of fresh meat, so I cannot attribute my relish of the roast of elk to the way it was served, or to a craving appetite, but the merit must have been in the meat itself. I was the more convinced of that after eating a broiled tenderloin steak of it for breakfast the next morning.

We learned that there had been a fall of snow where we encamped only a day or two before, but at noon-day the weather was then quite warm, though a couple of pairs of blankets were not undesirable articles on our beds at night.

Cool nights are characteristic of the plains, whether contiguous to the mountains as we then were or not. The season for musquitoes in that locality had not arrived, and our sleep was undisturbed and refreshing.

We passed several additional graves of soldiers and citizens murdered by the Indians the year before, and on the head-board of one I read, "*Burned by the Indians*," etc. Subsequently I learned the particulars of the death of the unfortunate man buried there. He was one of a small party of soldiers guarding a train which was attacked by the savages, and all his companions escaped, but he was captured. The inhuman wretches then tied him to the wheel of a wagon, loaded with combustible material, and set fire to it, burning the unfortunate soldier to a crisp. Horrible! but literally true!

Winding around the base of the mountain, in a westerly direction, in two or three days we reached the next military post—Fort Halleck.

CHAPTER VI.

FROM FORT HALLECK TO THE NORTH PLATTE.

Fort Halleck, another of the frontier posts established since the late war began, was a rudely built and unattractive station, situated at the base of the western part of the Medicine Bow range of mountains, or what is more commonly called the Elk Mountain. In this locality the most violent winter winds prevail, rendering it exceedingly bleak and uncomfortable for many months in the year. Fort Halleck has an elevation of nearly 8,000 feet above the sea, and on the 4th of July of last year was visited by a severe snow-storm. Since we passed there in the middle of June, the post has been discontinued, and the garrison removed 60 miles east, to a point in Laramie Plains, near where we crossed the Big Laramie River, to which I referred in my last.

Soon after our arrival there, the work of demolishing the

old station, and building the new, began. For the new post, a new name was adopted, and at first it was known as Fort John Buford, after one of the dead heroes of the late war, but since, the name has been changed again to Fort Sanders. The post was built under the personal supervision of Brevet Lieut.-Col. Mizner, of the 18th Infantry, who was a *compagnon du voyage* from St. Louis on the march I am now describing. Fort Sanders is probably the best post on the frontier, constructed solely by soldiers' labor, in the West.

The old site of Fort Halleck is in a section of country far removed from settlements, and frequented only by frontiersmen, Indians, bears, and the passing traveller, with here and there a ranche, the keepers of which are generally a rough, desperate-looking set of men, conforming with the character of the country in which they reside.

A total disregard of civil law prevails here; indeed, there are no civil officers to enforce law, and the bold perpetration of murder and other gross crimes has been of frequent occurrence. In many instances they pass unnoticed, but sometimes there are mock-trials and executions, by self-constituted courts, more barbarous in their character, than the bold assassinations for real and imaginary wrongs, which the courts are intended to punish. I was informed of one where a frontiersman was tried for murder, said to have been committed in self-defence, and while a jury of *four* men was hearing the evidence, a party were at work digging a grave and making a coffin for the prisoner, whose case had evidently been prejudged, and he was tried and executed all within a few hours. Everybody goes armed. A frontiersman would be more likely to forget or neglect to put on his hat when going out in a snow-storm, than to leave behind him his pistol on any occasion. They place a very low value on human life, and to shoot a man dead because of a slight controversy, is considered the most expeditious and certain way of settling the misunderstanding.

A vigilance committee exists in the territory, but without

the organization and concert of action which characterized the great California committee in the early part of the history of that State.

The conduct of some of the "vigilanters," as they are called, has been so represented to me, that I would about as lief meet in an unfrequented place, an old grizzly, or two or three hostile Sioux, as one of these protectors (?) of the peace of the territory.

Considering all things, I congratulated myself upon not being ordered to a post in that country, preferring to take the chances of a more congenial state of things at a more distant station.

The prices charged for such articles as could be purchased of the sutler at Halleck, or at the ranches in the vicinity, were enormously high. The canned fruits and vegetables for which I paid $3 and $4 a dozen in Leavenworth, $2 a can was here the lowest price, and flour, for which an officer would be charged 5 cents a pound by the Commissary, was sold to the emigrant by the sutler in an adjoining building at 60 cents, while shot for which I paid 15 cents a pound in St. Louis, here commanded 75 cents; and this enormous advance is charged, when the highest rate of freight from the Missouri River is 12 cents per pound. I was glad to find that my larder required no further replenishing than the Commissary could supply.

At Fort Halleck our column was still further reduced by turning over to that garrison two other companies, and there we parted with another of our Surgeons, Dr. Avery, leaving but one, of about a dozen that left Leavenworth, to continue the journey. But there was little need for doctors. It is astonishing how healthy men keep when on a march. We did not leave a single sick man at any post between Leavenworth and Salt Lake City.

A two days' march from Halleck brought us to the ferry of the North Platte. As we descended into the valley the roadside was literally covered with wild flowers, varied in kind and color to an extent we had not before observed. They were of varieties different from any cultivated flowers

I have seen, and of an exquisite beauty of form and color that would rival the rarest productions in the conservatories of our eastern cities.

But from this scene of life and beauty we must take the reader to one of a different character. Reaching the river we found it swollen, its current of unusual swiftness, and a strong wind blowing so as to render it hazardous to attempt a crossing, and for a day or two we remained in camp, awaiting more auspicious circumstances. The wind having subsided the crossing commenced, and the entire supply train got over without accident, and then began the ferrying over of the wagons with company baggage. Soon after this commenced, through the carelessness of the ferryman, who had been indulging freely in whiskey, the boat, with wagon, mules, and a number of men on it, swamped, just after leaving the shore, emptying everything into the rapid current. It was a shocking sight to behold. The men, mules and wagon were rushed by within a few yards of the shore, and hundreds witnessed the scene, but were unable to render any assistance to their drowning comrades, who sunk beneath the surface, one after another, right before our eyes, until five had drowned. A few escaped, including the ferryman, but the mules, wagon and contents were all lost.

I had crossed previous to the accident and witnessed on the western bank an affecting scene. The wife and child of a sergeant who was among the lost, saw the accident from where I stood, but were not aware of the husband and father being on the boat, until the report was made from the other side that Serg't St. John was drowned. The grief of the widow was then demonstrated in the most bitter weeping, while the little girl of about 10 years became almost frantic, uttered the most piteous shrieks, and had to be forcibly restrained from rushing into the frightful stream. I have but seldom witnessed a sight more affecting! The child continued in this highly agitated state until nearly exhausted, and then in the most deliberate manner clasped her hands together, raised her eyes, and with beautiful emphasis, exclaimed: "Good Lord, have mercy upon me, and help me to bear this." The prayer seemed to bring its immediate answer, for the little one was quiet at once and appeared reconciled, and afterward exhibited much fortitude.

No other boat was to be had, and the larger part of the command had not crossed, and were separated from supplies which were on the western side. Nothing could be got over, and wagons were sent back to Fort Halleck for subsistence for the men until the ferry could be reëstablished.

The boat, which had landed on an island two miles below was, after great exertion by the entire command, recovered and brought back to the ferry, but not until another life was lost in the attempt—the proprietor of a freight train, who was assisting the soldiers in getting the boat from the island to the mainland, was drowned within ten feet of the bank of the stream. He was a wealthy and highly respected citizen of Nebraska.

This ferry is the property of the Overland Mail Company, of which Mr. Ben Holladay was then the principal stockholder. Indeed, he might be said to own the line between the Missouri River and Salt Lake City, so complete was his control of it. I will take this occasion to refer again to this company, as I promised to do in a previous letter.

A few years ago Mr. Holladay contracted with the Post-Office Department to run a daily mail from the Missouri river to the Pacific. For doing so, he was to receive from the Government *seven hundred and fifty thousand dollars a year*; and various military posts were established along the route, both for the protection of the mails and the property of the contractor. Wherever there was danger of a coach being attacked by Indians, a military escort accompanied it. The mail is carried in the boots of stage-coaches, which are patronized by passengers at all seasons; and the coaches also carry express packages, for which freight at the rate of one dollar per pound is charged to Salt Lake City. For a through trip to California, at the time Mr. H. relinquished control of the line, a ticket cost about *four hundred and fifty dollars*—meals extra, at the rate of a dollar to a dollar and a half each, and for all baggage in excess of 25 lbs., a dollar and a half per pound is charged. He has been reimbursed by the Government for animals lost or stolen by the Indians, and since the contract for carrying the mails was awarded to him, he has secured the passage by Congress of a bill, *requiring letter postage to be paid* on all printed matter sent in the overland mail, except on newspapers mailed by the publishers to regular subscribers. Fond mothers are thus deprived of the privilege of sending occasionally a newspaper to a soldier son on the frontier, and sweethearts in the States must content themselves by writing to their soldier lovers the gist of the new novels, as it is too expensive to forward them in Mr. Holladay's mail.

How has the Government, which has sustained this monopoly, been treated in return for its liberality?

It is the custom of railroad companies, throughout the States, to transport officers and soldiers of the army over their lines, on orders of quartermasters, for which they collect a lower rate than is charged passengers generally. Mr. Holladay refuses to recognize the orders of a quartermaster, because, when settling his last account, he was required to make a deduction from the enormous rates charged. No officer or soldier is allowed to travel in his coaches without paying for a ticket at the established rate. The result of this was great inconvenience to officers, and injury to the service. For instance, an officer may be ordered from Camp Douglas to Fort Leavenworth; he has not $300 to meet his expenses, but he must go. The quartermaster then furnishes him with an ambulance and wagon, and the commanding officers of posts escort him through the dangerous country, and after a two months' journey he reaches his destination, the Government having incurred greater expense than the stage-fare, besides losing the officer's services for the two months he spent on the way.

The mail company have made ferries, and built bridges over streams crossed by their coaches. When government teams pass over these ferries or bridges, the same rates of toll or ferriage are charged as to emigrants—indeed higher rates if the cash is not paid. At the North Platte a traveller might cross a single wagon for five dollars, and if the Government crossed a hundred, the ferryman would require a voucher for seven dollars a wagon—that is, two dollars additional for sending to Denver to collect. On the occasion of the accident referred to, after the loss of six lives, and a large amount of public property, through the carelessness of an employe, and the labor of several hundred soldiers in recovering the lost boat, and re-establishing the ferry, an agent of the company thought the Government should pay something, if not full ferriage. Most decidedly cool!

The stages at both termini of the route are fine Concord coaches; but these seldom get beyond the first home station, when inferior ones are substituted, and both stages and stock continue depreciating as you go onward, and on some parts of the route the passengers often, in bad weather, are compelled to walk for miles, because of the horses being unable to draw them. I have in several instances known passengers to be transferred from the inferior coaches, commonly known on the plains as "mud wagons," to a common army-wagon, without springs or cover.

Mr. Colfax and party, when crossing the continent, were furnished one of the best coaches, and that allowed to go all the way through, hence Mr. Bowles' unqualified praise of their conveyances. If the party had travelled incog., and been transferred into an uncovered army-wagon, it would probably have interfered very materially with Mr. Holladay's influence in the House of Representatives.

There are some of the facts connected with the stage company as conducted a few months ago. Since that time it has passed into the hands of the enterprising and popular firm of Wells, Fargo & Co., who are now the proprietors of the line through to the Pacific, having some time previously purchased the line from Salt Lake City west. One of the first acts of the new company was to reduce the fare, and I understand the line has already grown in popularity.*

While awaiting the recovery of the boat, and the crossing of the remainder of the command over the North Platte, those of us on the western side were visited by a large band of the Ute Indians, who had come down the road to trade skins and furs before going on the war-path against the Arapahoes with whom they are at enmity. Their squaws, old men and pappooses had all been left behind, and the entire band was mounted on ponies, and armed. Their ostensible mission, as I said before, was a fight with the Arapahoes, but I was much inclined to the belief that they were really on a grand stealing expedition, and a little extra vigilance was exercised in guarding our animals. They traded large numbers of beaver skins and dressed buckskins to the officers and soldiers for old coats, blankets, &c., but seemed to place no value on greenbacks. Hardly from a want of confidence in the stability of the Government! I exhibited to one who was above the average in point of intelligence a fifty dollar bill, and at the same time a new ten cent note; the latter he seemed to regard as the most desirable, but would not accept either in trade for a beaver skin, which he afterward bartered away for an old cast-off woolen shirt. Many of them exhibited shrewdness in trading, and I think understood English better than they were willing to admit. They were exceedingly anxious to trade for weapons and ammunition, but further than a few cartridges, which the soldiers bartered away, they got nothing of the kind.

Throughout the journey it was a rule with officers not to leave the column or camp without means of defence against Indians; and indeed at nearly all times I had my pistol by my side ready for an emergency. One afternoon, however, when lying in my tent, I removed the weapon and put it

---

*Since the above was written a gentleman informed me that he had seen a copy of a letter addressed by the Postmaster General, to Mr. Holladay, calling his attention to frequent neglects to comply with his contracts notwithstanding the great liberality of the Government, and threatening to cancel the contract if not more carefully regarded.

under my pillow, and being called to visit an emigrant camp a short distance off, I rode out alone, and turning suddenly around a hill, I came upon two of the most desperate and villainous-looking warriors I had seen in the band. As they started to accompany me, all riding abreast, I discovered that I had left my pistol behind, and it being desirable, under the circumstances, to appear as friendly as possible, with the most complacent smile I could make I gave the usual salutation "How." This was recognized by a sort of grunt, like a dog, by the fellow next to me, with any other than a pleasant expression of countenance, and his want of cordiality was not the less noticed because of a long lance which he carried in his hand. I may have been in no danger, but must confess to some degree of nervousness, and breathed more freely when I came up with a few emigrants after a very short and very unpleasant ride with my dusty companions.

The Utes, I understand, have not been hostile to emigrants generally, but are unfriendly toward the Mormons, and have commttied depredations upon their trains and other property, and charge the "saints" with deceitfulness and treachery. A queer charge coming from an Indian!

During our stay upon the Platte they encamped on the bluffs all around us; and notwithstanding their protestations of friendship and the absence of all hostility on their part for some years, I had so little confidence in the Indian character that I could have slept more soundly if a little further removed from so large a number of armed warriors. Their weapons consisted of a great variety, including rifles, shot-guns, pistols, lances, and bows and arrows, but the latter predominated.

After a delay of six days the command was crossed without further accident, and we resumed our marches over a mountainous country, reaching Bridger's Pass in two days. This was an epoch of our journey, for we had reached the western slope of the Rocky Mountains.

CHAPTER VII.

FROM BRIDGER'S PASS TO GREEN RIVER.

TRAVELLING along a deep valley, with tall mountains on either side, we leave a small stream which runs eastward, finally to empty into the Gulf of Mexico, and in a few minutes come to another that flows into the great Pacific. This valley is the celebrated Bridger's Pass in the Rocky Mountains.

Though at an elevation of 8,000 feet, quite a change in the appearance of things was to be observed at once. The grass was more luxuriant and the snow-capped mountains had now disappeared, and those around us were covered with verdure to their summits. All nature seemed to wear a more genial aspect, and we travelled forward anticipating still further evidences of a more temperate climate. The weather grew warmer, and we were subjected to the annoyance of myriads of mosquitoes, which were vastly more troublesome than they ever proved to be in New Orleans. They not only bit the exposed skin, but through the thinner clothing, and an ordinary glove afforded no protection to the hands. The horses became victims as well as their riders, and soon their bodies were covered with great lumps from the irritation of the bite of these troublesome little insects. In camp we resorted to the almost suffocating smoke from a smudge of sage-brush to drive them from our tents; but fortunately the cool nights caused them to disappear soon after sundown.

For days before the time of which I now write, as well

as for weeks afterward, we were almost constantly meeting the trains of emigrants returning from California. It was surprising to witness this great tide of emigration from the Land of Gold back to the Eastern States. Hundreds of families, with all their wordly goods and their entire households, were seeking again the homes of their earlier years.

I have often heard of the Pacific coast as being most prolific in its multiplication of the *genus homo*, but I never fully realized the extent to which the "blessings" and "responsibilities" of the Californian might be increased until I saw these trains. "A poor man for children," is an old vulgar adage, but I would substitute for it, "A Californian for children." We passed wagon after wagon with juvenile heads in front, juvenile heads behind, juvenile heads to the right, and juvenile heads to the left—literally rows of little faces, from two to a dozen years old, peeping out from under the covers all around, and all dirty, healthy, and happy.

I inquired the cause of this great exodus from a land into which, only a few years ago, over the same road, the gold-seeking travellers poured like pilgrims into Mecca, and learned that California now is the gold-field only for Chinamen and capitalists. Gold is still abundant in extensive quartz ledges, but is fast disappearing from the beds of streams, where a few years ago so much was obtained by the miner with his pick, shovel, and wash-pan. Extensive machinery is required in mining profitably the ledges to which I refer, and these ledges are now monopolized by capitalists with their immense quartz-crushing and hydraulic mining machines, and the yield of gold from them, though as great perhaps as ever from quartz mining, is now divided among the few instead of the masses, as formerly. The primitive mode of mining has ceased to be profitable to all save "John Chinaman," who toils hard in the almost exhausted "diggings" for a very small quantity of gold; and his frugality is such that he will save money where even the prudent Yankee would starve. The latter, therefore, are fast abandoning the country, either to search for the precious metal in Idaho or Montana, where it abounds in the beds of streams, as formerly in California, or to return to their homes, as was the case with those we met. They informed me that there were thousands of families who remained in the State only because of a want of means to enable them to leave it.

Disappointed miners were not confined to those of California only, but the newer regions had theirs also. About the time of which I have been writing, I met the very extensive effects of a defunct mining company returning from the new gold region of Montana. It consisted of a train of elaborately constructed wagons, on which the bright red paint was yet comparatively fresh, and conspicuously lettered upon each was "Montana U. S. Gold Mining Co." With them were a large engine and boilers, and the whole was en route for Denver City, where the effects of the company had been sold. I got the following bit of history from the gentleman in charge of the train.

Some time ago some shrewd individuals from Montana called upon capitalists in the East, and portrayed, in very extravagant terms, the immense wealth of gold lands where they represented that they had established claims; but for want of means were unable to work the mines successfully on their own account. They exhibited specimens of rich gold quartz, with elaborate charts of the country in which the gold lands were represented to be located. Without a survey of the country, or inspection of the mines, and entirely upon the representations of these men, a company, with a capital of $200,000, was immediately organized, and the outfit to which I have referred was the result. After a year's explorations and researches, not only did they fail to produce the gold which they expected to pour like a stream into their treasury, *but were unable to find even the land they had purchased.*

This may strike the reader as an improbable story, but I give it upon the authority of an intelligent gentleman who was in charge of the property.

I find that I have digressed widely, and much of the space allowed for this week's letter I have filled in writing about things, though not entirely irrelevant, certainly not descriptive of my journey.

In passing through the Rocky Mountains, I observed at various places thick strata of coal cropping out along the declivities, and here and there I found small mines, worked by the Overland Stage Company, for supplying a cheap fuel for the stations in the vicinity. The coal obtained is of a bituminous nature, and resembles much the celebrated cannel coal of England. In the same section of country, exuding from the crevices in the rocks, was a dark, semi-liquid substance, having the appearance and physical properties of petroleum, and I have no doubt was such in reality. This very much excited a brother officer, who might be said to have "petroleum on the brain." He indulged in many visionary schemes of making great wealth from oil-wells in the Rocky Mountains. When the great Pacific Railroad shall have been completed to these mountains, the materials for running the road will be conveniently at hand, and at the same time the immense mineral resources of this region will be developed. Had I the hidden wealth contained in the mountains I had passed thus far on my journey in an Eastern market, I think I might afford to pay one-half of the national debt, and retire from the army to a life of affluence.

After passing beyond the mountains, we came upon an extensive barren plain abounding in wild-sage bushes, which grew to a height of three or four feet. There were hundreds of thousands of acres of this land with no other vegetable growth upon it, and because of its peculiar production it is known as the Artemesian Plain—Artemesia being the botanical name of the sage which covers it everywhere. So large were the bushes that it afforded a very convenient firewood (all to be had), and was objectionable as such only because of the unpleasant smell about the camp occasioned by its combustion.

A few days' march over this country brought us to a tributary of Green River—a small disgusting stream, known as Bitter Creek. This was the first bad water we had been compelled to use since leaving the Big Muddy, south of Fort Kearney. It was a small sluggish stream, changing the color of its water with that of the soil through which it flowed, and in some places looked like a mucilage of red brick-dust. Its name is owing to an alkaline rather than bitter taste, caused by the absorption of a substance of that nature of which I have spoken as abounding in the soil of most of this western country. There were frequent reports by emigrants of its fatal effects upon animals that drank of it, but I failed to observe any unpleasant consequences either to the animal man or of the brute creation, both of which classes in our command and train drank of it freely, on a march of several days.

Of all the country we marched over between Leavenworth and Salt Lake City, that along Bitter Creek was the most barren and uninviting. On the prairies of Kansas, along the valleys of the Platte, and Lodge Pole Creek, in the Black Hills, on Laramie Plain, through Bridger's Pass, everywhere else I saw something to admire; but along Bitter Creek is an arid waste, without a redeeming feature. It was disgusting to travel through the country at any time, but seemed particularly so on Independence Day. Grass for the animals was scarce, the water bad, the weather hot and dry, the dust thick—in a word, everything conspired to disgust the traveller, and even some of our mules became demoralized, and strayed off in search of a more congenial country. When I pass along Bitter Creek again I hope it will be at night in a sleeping-car.

One day, while passing along this part of our route, I observed a man at one of the stage stations preparing for a hunting excursion, and upon inquiry I learned that he was employed by the company to hunt game for them, and received for his services the value of the meat he brought in. This hunter had been captain in a volunteer regiment, and when mustered out of service decided to remain a year in the country to indulge in the sport of hunting large game, such as deer, elk and bear, and found this a way of combining profit with amusement. On his excursions he would go alone, taking two horses, one of which he rode and on the other he packed his game to bring in, and was usually absent only two days in securing a load for his pack-animal. From this employment he realized the handsome sum of about $300 a month. It is only an experienced hunter and a good shot, however, who could make it so profitable. I regretted that I could not leave the command for a hunt with him, but that was impracticable, and I had to forego the pleasure of shooting an elk or a bear until a more convenient season, if such ever occurs, and it has not up to the date of this writing.

We met on this part of our journey several droves of California horses, on their way to the States. These animals are purchased on the Pacific coast, at a very low rate, and are driven across the plains at a season when grass is good, and their transfer to a more profitable market is thus attended with but slight expense. If the Indians should run off a herd or two it would require several trips to make good the loss. The California horse is not so large or so hardy as our eastern horses, which always command a very high price west of the mountains. They are known there as the American horse, in contradistinction from the California horse, or the Indian horse, which is a native of the plains or mountains.

As we marched along Bitter Creek, toward its mouth, our route was over a much less elevated country than that through which we had marched from Fort Halleck westward through Bridger's Pass, and it being the second week in July the weather had become oppressively hot during the middle of the day. But in what remarkable contrast with the sensations of our skin was the sight we beheld when looking both to the north and to the south! For several days we had lost sight of snow-clad mountains, but again they came in view, and more of them than we had seen at one time before. Far away to the north were the Wind River Mountains—say 60 or 70 miles distant—their summits completely covered with snow, and their outlines as distinct as similar eminences would appear in the atmosphere of Louisiana at one-twelfth the distance. At the most remote part of the range towered up the lofty Fremont's Peak, whose summit reaches an altitude of more than 13,000 feet above that of New Orleans. To the south could be observed with equal distinctness the range of the Uintah Mountains, likewise white with snow.

We are now supposed to have reached the mouth of Bitter Creek, about which I have said such bitter things in this letter, and in my next we will resume our march from Green River, westward.

CHAPTER VIII.

FROM GREEN RIVER TO FORT BRIDGER.

GREEN RIVER is a stream of considerable importance. It rises in the Wind River Mountains, in the western part of Idaho Territory, and flowing south and west through Utah, becomes the Rio Colorado in Arizona, and empties into the Gulf of California. Green River is not navigable, or rather, it has never been navigated, and there is a very great difference of opinion as to whether it can be or not. The Colorado has been navigated, and is still, in the lower part of its course. I understand attempts are to be made next summer to run steamers far up into Green River. Some are of the opinion that this stream can be navigated as high as the mouth of Bitter Creek; but those who are most familiar with it think it entirely impracticable. I am very well satisfied that it is impracticable after hearing the arguments, pro and con. During the greater part of the year there are many places where the water is not over six or eight inches deep, the stream being very wide, and in other places it is narrow, and so filled with rocks and boulders that a yawl-boat could hardly pass safely between them. In the spring and early summer months there is unquestionably water enough at such places to float a small steamer; but at such times an equally formidable difficulty presents itself in the swiftness of the current.*

Green River takes its name from the green foliage along its banks, which in many parts of its course appear in remarkable contrast with the sterile land contiguous to them. Like all the mountain streams we crossed it was much swollen by the melted snow, and through its somewhat narrow bed at the point where the road strikes it, its current was exceedingly rapid. It was not fordable, and the ferry, during the early summer months, yields a handsome profit to the Overland Stage Company, by whom it is owned. As usual, the ferriage was enormously high, and there is no way of evading the extortion to which the passing trains are subjected.

This, like all the other ferries over the rapid streams of the West, is constructed and worked at a very slight expense to the owners. A description of it may not be uninteresting to the reader. There is stretched across the stream, a few feet above the water, a stout rope cable, to which a rudely constructed flat-boat, capable of carrying over a four-horse wagon, is attached by ropes at either end, passing through pulleys which slide along the cable. When the boat is about to cross the rope, the forward end is drawn in so as to make that end approach the cable, and the one at the hinder part is slackened so that the side of the boat will be brought obliquely against the current. The force of the water then propels it forward, upon the same principle that

* Since the above was written, there has been published in the Denver and Salt Lake papers, a letter written by Bvt. Lt.-Col. Mills, in command of Fort Bridger, in which he states that he proposes to apply to the War Department for authority to explore the river next summer. The Colonel thinks a small steamer, with engines of more than ordinary power, can safely navigate the stream to within a short distance of his post. The Colonel's letter to the contrary notwithstanding, I am still of the opinion expressed above.

the wind striking obliquely the sails of a vessel gives it an onward motion, or the flat surface of the boy's kite elevates it in the air. When the boat has crossed, its position to the current is simply reversed by tightening the rope at the opposite end and slackening it where it was tight, and what was the stern becomes the bow, and it recrosses the stream by the same propelling power. One or two men only are required to manage a loaded boat, and the rapidity of its motion through the water would astonish one who has never witnessed the operation.

We crossed Green River without a repetition of the horrible accident that occurred on the North Platte a short time before. Our thoughtful commanding officer took the precaution to substitute a stouter rope, which was in the train, for the somewhat frail-looking one which spanned the river when we reached the ferry; but altogether the crossing was more carefully managed, and there was no indulgence in whiskey-drinking by the ferrymen when so many lives were intrusted to their care. Similar carelessness, notwithstanding the precautions taken, would doubtless have resulted in a similar catastrophe to the one on the Platte.

The next locality that attracted our attention was a small trading settlement on "Ham's Fork," a stream emptying into Green River.

A few white men, and a larger number of Indians and half-breeds, all living in lodges, earn a livelihood at this place by buying and selling cattle. When an ox becomes foot-sore and exhausted on his long journey, the alternative with the owner lays between abandoning his animal or selling him for what he can get, and under these circumstances such traders purchase for a mere nominal sum, and after a few weeks' rest the ox is sold again for a high price. The amount of money made in this way on the plains is by no means insignificant. These men also trade with the Indians, after they return from their yearly hunts, for robes and skins, which they obtain at a mere trifling cost, and then sell them on the spot for a higher price than the same articles would command in St. Louis.

It has been the practice of thieving Indians, almost yearly, to fall upon the cattle belonging to the traders at this post and run them off. On the night of our encampment there a rumor prevailed that a band of Indians was in the vicinity on such a mission, and no little excitement occurred in consequence. Every animal belonging to the traders was driven in from the grazing ground, and the Colonel furnished a guard for the protection of the settlement; but the rumor proved to be false, and the guard was withdrawn in the morning, when we continued our march.

This is a great country for "Forks." We have a Ham's, a Smith's, a Henry's, and we soon reached another—Black's—and then encamped. We were then in a more attractive, and what might be made a fertile and productive country. The banks of the stream were covered with wild roses, and tall rich grass took the place of sage-brush, very much to the gratification of the mules, for they had not had such grazing since we left Lodge Pole Creek.

A remarkable natural curiosity in this vicinity is "Church Butte," a tall mound of soft sandstone and clay, which has been shaped by the winds and rains in this very muddy country, so as to present the appearance of the ruins of a vast gothic cathedral. Its towers and porch and pillars may be as distinctly traced as if the ruins of ancient masonry. Such winds as prevail here I might expect to blow anything into, or out of shape; but I could hardly conceive it possible that such a grand object could be formed as it has been. Far above its steeple-like summits, was once the surface of this whole country around, but it has been gradually levelled, by the hand of time and the elements, and the butte, being a part more capable of resistance than the earth around it, remains a beautiful natural monument. The formation of the butte is of soft sandstone and its shape changes from year to year; but those who saw it many years ago say it is not less remarkable now than it was when they first saw it.

Along the road in this vicinity are found some very beautiful specimens of the moss agate, a variety of translucent quartz, with what appear as little sprigs of moss imbedded in it. These little moss-like particles are deposits of oxide of iron, which take place during the formation of the stone. The best specimens are highly prized for jewelry. Obtaining a very pretty fragment, I sent it to California to be cut, and set in a ring. I was quite surprised at the difference made in the appearance of the stone by polishing. As found, it was quite opaque; but when returned in the ring, it was almost transparent. I shall preserve this as a memento of a trip across the Rocky Mountains.

One day's march from Church Butte, and we were at Fort Bridger, which is the oldest military station passed on the march, save Fort Kearney. The site is that of a former trading-post of an old mountaineer of the name the Fort now bears. He has long been known to officers of the army on the frontier as a guide and interpreter. The present military post was established in 1858, after the arrival of Gen. Albert Sidney's Johnston's expedition against the Mormons. It is situated 120 miles east of Salt Lake City, and the immediate site of the Fort is a locality occupied by Brigham Young and his followers when seeking their new Zion in Salt Lake Valley in 1847. A tall stone wall—a parallelogram in shape—built by the Mormons for protection against the Indians, still stands just below the parade ground. Black's Fork, to which I have before alluded as a tributary of Green River, rises in the Uintah Mountains, and before reaching the Fort divides into five branches, one of which passes directly through the post, affording an abundant supply of clear, cool, and the most delicious water, fresh from the mountain springs. About a mile below the post these branches unite again and form one stream, thence to the river where it empties. The fort is located in an extensive basin, surrounded by a succession of table-lands, rising one above the other, which are styled "benches." These benches are so level, and their slope so regular, that when observed from a short distance, they appear not unlike an embankment for a railroad over a low flat country. The soil on the surface of this entire section of

FORT BRIDGER. OFFICERS' QUARTERS.

country is alluvium, and it bears other evidences of having been once the bottom of an inland sea. From any of the benches the Fort presents a neat and attractive appearance. After passing through what appeared an almost interminable region of sage-brush and grease-wood, the beautiful green of the small cotton-wood and willow trees, and the more beautiful wild roses then in full bloom on the banks of a little stream which runs by the side of the road leading to the Fort, made the spot appear a very desirable one for an officer's station, were it not for its isolated position.

This post was built by an officer no where better known or more highly appreciated for his sterling qualities than in New Orleans. I refer to Gen. Canby. The quarters are constructed of hewn logs, and those of the officers neatly plastered and provided with such conveniences as to afford a comfortable home to those who have to occupy them.

In the vicinity game is abundant. The sage-hen—the largest known bird of the grouse family—are said to be more numerous here than in any part of the West. I have seen some almost the size of an ordinary wild turkey. Not many miles distant deer and elk are to be found, while the streams are full of the most beautiful brook trout, weighing from half a pound to a pound and a half. To an officer fond of hunting or fishing, the sport here afforded must in a great measure recompense for the want of society and little inconveniences incident to life at such a remote station; and, indeed, taking all things in consideration, I felt like congratulating those who were to remain, for I considered it preferable to any post we passed on the route.

Along our journey I made frequent inquiries of those I met concerning the military stations as we approached them; and whenever I conversed with an individual who could give me any information about Fort Bridger, I was almost certain to hear during the conversation some such remark as the following: "And you will find Judge Carter, the sutler, there, and a finer gentleman you never met." We met the Judge and he proved to be all that had been represented. Judge Carter is Probate Judge of the County, and came to this country with the army of Gen. Johnston, and has been the sutler at Fort Bridger since its establishment. For thirty years he has been with the army, and I found him a perfect encyclopedia of information concerning it. Mention the name of an officer of the old army and he will give you his whole history. We found him a high-toned, intelligent, and hospitable Virginia gentleman, universally popular with all who associated with him, and deservedly so. His store contains a larger assortment of every variety of goods and wares than any similar establishment west of the Missouri River. I was informed by good authority, that his purchases in the East last year amounted to $180,000. This large trade is by no means confined to those at the post, but is principally with miners and emigrants. His success in business has doubtless surpassed his most sanguine expectations.

I have seldom met with a more hospitable gentleman than Judge Carter, and there is always a plate at his table for a visitor at the post or a passing friend, the pleasure of entertaining a guest is the only remuneration he will receive for his liberality, be the entertained friend or stranger.

Living on the reservation is another character, almost as generally known as the Judge. I refer to an old trader and mountaineer named Robinson, but passing always under the sobriquet of "Uncle Jack." He has been living on the frontier for nearly forty years, and has adopted many of the habits of the aborigines, several of whom he has as wives. During the summer months his abode is an Indian lodge, and in the winter he is ensconced in a log cabin, a few miles from the fort. Uncle Jack, though for so many years without the bounds of civilization, has acquired none of that rudeness of manner, which it would seem must always necessarily follow his associations and mode of life. He is always polite, kind in his feelings, and very entertaining in his conversation, having an exhaustless fund of incidents in the life of a mountaineer. He is generous, also, to a fault, and has accommodated persons with cattle and money amounting to many thousands of dollars, of which he will never receive a dime. There are always about his premises, from six to a dozen persons, not connected with his family (a few Indians always included), who live at his expense. Persons who know him intimately say he never complains of such imposition, and when advised by friends to send away such loafers, he always has some ready excuse for their idleness, and expresses the hope that they will soon be able to earn something wherewith to pay for their board. There are scores and hundreds of just such worthless indolent people scattered throughout the Far West. Some of the men have their families with them, and those who have not usually take squaws, and they eat and sleep away a miserable existence, apparently without any object in life.

As may have been inferred from what I have said already, Uncle Jack is a *natural gentleman*—one of those noble characters who have the instincts and feelings of gentlemen, place them where you may. His associations and habits may degrade him, but you will always find cropping out those qualities which indicate him as intended for a different sphere in life, and mark what he would have been under different circumstances.

Uncle Jack is now sixty-five years old, but is hale and hearty, though of course not so active as in early life. He has an iron constitution, and has passed through enough to break even that, I should think. He is exceedingly fond of his toddy, or the toddy minus the water and sugar. A gentleman told me that eight years ago he saw him take *ten* drinks of whiskey before breakfast, apparently without feeling the effects of them. But now it requires comparatively little to produce intoxication. He says it is ridiculous to talk about *bad whiskey*—that there is no such thing; some whiskey he pronounces better than others, but says he never saw any *bad* whiskey. If the reader could taste, or smell, some of the stuff distilled in this country, and known as "Valley Tan," he would rather doubt Uncle Jack's qualifications as a "taster" for a liquor-store. He advises Judge Carter to bring out a distillery next year—thinks there is a great waste of the raw material in making corn and wheat into bread, as it would go much further if converted into a liquid. I said to him one day,

"Uncle Jack, is the water in Smith's Fork (where he lives) as good as we have it here in Black's?"

"Indeed, sir, I can't tell you. I don't drink water. I never tasted it. You see, sir, I am getting old, and it might freeze up in me."

But such remarks as these are made only to amuse a convivial party. He would never indulge in such to a stranger, or to any one, unless encouraged to do so.

He has made a good deal of money trading with Indians and emigrants, and years ago at trapping, but has lost a good deal, also. His means, however, are sufficient to support him comfortably for the balance of his life; and while he owns a farm in Missouri, he is so well pleased with his present way of living, that he prefers to end his days on the frontier, notwithstanding the urgent appeal of relatives in the States to spend his declining years where he can have more of the comforts of life.

CHAPTER IX

MORE ABOUT FORT BRIDGER, AND A RIDE IN A SNOW-STORM.

THE Government reservation upon which Fort Bridger is located (there are always reserves about military posts), is twenty-five miles square, and embraces some of the richest and most desirably-located lands for agricultural purposes that I have seen on the western slope of the Rocky Mountains. Some parts of it are now cultivated by the sutler, who has permission to do so from the War Department, and his crops demonstrate clearly the productiveness of the soil. The great drawback to this, as an agricultural country, is the shortness of the seasons, and the very uncertain weather of the spring and early autumn. Garden vegetables cannot be cultivated with much hope of uniform success. Some seasons, as the last, for instance, are so favorable, that almost any vegetable raised in Ohio might be raised here; but the probability is that for several succeeding years the late and early frosts would destroy all that might be planted. The sutler now confines his crops to oats and hay; and even his oat crop was a failure in '65, though the yield is so large, that if a ready sale could be made at the present rates, the failure of an entire crop every fourth year would still make it profitable farming.

The Bridger reservation has other resources than agricultural. Three miles from the Fort may be quarried, in any quantity desired, a silicious limestone well adapted for building purposes. As found, it is in regular layers of uniform thickness, and the great blocks or slabs, as taken from the quarry, look as if they had been wrought into shape by the chisel and mallet of the mason. When first removed, the stone is soft, and very easily dressed, but on exposure to the weather for a short time, becomes very hard. There are already several buildings at this post partially constructed of this stone; and Major Grimes, the Post Quartermaster at Camp Douglas, who is also Supervising Quartermaster at this post, has submitted to the Quartermaster-General, plans and specifications for a very elaborate garrison to be built of it.

Iron ore is found in the vicinity, and perhaps abounds on the reservation; and coal likewise. About twenty miles distant is a large flowing spring of petroleum, with indications of its existence in unlimited quantities in the country around. Within two miles of the post are large beds of gypsum, which might be easily calcined and converted into plaster of Paris on the spot; and about twelve miles to the south is a forest of heavy timber. Almost the entire reservation might be irrigated from the two streams that run through it, while these streams could also be turned to account, by furnishing water-power for mills.

The reader will inquire why a country with so many resources is not settled. The reason is, because the most desirable of it is not open for settlement, but included in the large reservation. Various inspecting officers have already recommended that this reservation be cut down. If it should be done, and the land thrown open for pre-emption, and a colony of industrious Germans, or any other thrifty people locate here, a few years would make a great change in the present desolate country. The passage of the Pacific Railroad through this valley or vicinity, would be another valuable stimulus to the development of the country. Anticipating this, Judge Carter has already established a saw-mill, and talks of bringing out another this year.

Fort Bridger, upon our arrival, was garrisoned by three companies of ex-rebel soldiers, who enlisted in our army, when prisoners of war, for duty on the frontier, fighting Indians. These troops are styled officially U. S. Volunteers, but are more generally known as "Galvanized Yankees," a term that seemed not at all offensive to them. The post had been most shamefully abused. Troops that had been mustered out of service shortly before our arrival, must have destroyed property from the mere desire to destroy; but in some instances there was apparently a little utility in their destructiveness, as they demolished buildings for firewood. Many of the officers just on the eve of leaving service, winked at the vandalism of their men, while others were unable to control them, if they had any desire to do so.

Everybody in this section of country seemed to have become completely demoralized. Citizens and soldiers were alike in this respect. Some of the latter were so regarded in the eastern armies, and became ten times worse when they were sent on the plains against their wishes. Men stole and officers stole! That is their own testimony. I was not here to judge for myself; but I have known individuals who formerly held commissions, give to each other the worst of characters. I might one day meet a former Capt. A, and he would tell me that Capt B, when Quartermaster, swindled the Government out of thousands, by fraudulent vouchers. The next day, perchance, I might meet the former Capt. B, and he would tell me that Capt. A, when Commissary of Subsistence, was the greatest scoundrel in Utah—that he robbed the Government of bacon and flour enough to last his family for five years, &c. The third day I might meet the two together, and they would both unite in telling about how Capt. C stole wagon tires and chains to fix his mill in Rush Valley, and sold Government horses to himself for a mere song. One officer would wilfully deceive another, apparently for the morbid pleasure he would take in getting him in trouble, and then tell it as a good joke.

Disciplined troops and honest officers were not sent to this country any too soon; and I fancy that Major Burt, when he assumed command at Fort Bridger, had not the easiest task in the world in attempting to straighten out things. I must in justice to some of the late officers remark, that they were not all of this class, by any means. Several that I have met have proved themselves to be gentlemen, and honored the positions they held.

The locality of Fort Bridger was made a memorable one to me on an occasion subsequent to the march I am describing, and I will here make another gap in my narrative to refer to the event, and record an exciting adventure in a snow-storm.

On a clear bright morning in the month of October a party of seven, three ladies, a little son of one of them, and three gentlemen, including myself, started from Camp Douglas for Fort Bridger, on a pleasure trip. When we started the temperature, as well as the hazy appearance of the atmosphere over the whole valley, indicated that delightful season, Indian Summer, which is so much enjoyed on the Atlantic coast, and elsewhere in the States. Being rather thickly clad, before entering the mountain pass I removed my vest as necessary for comfort. Travelling in ambulances, as we did, without a change of horses, it is a three-days' journey. Before completing the first, however, we were so much higher, and the temperature so much lower, that I not only returned my vest, but found an overcoat quite a desirable addition to my clothing. The second day was cold, damp, cloudy, and altogether very disagreeable. And as we started on the third, the clouds still hung about the mountains, and had already deposited on the range to the south a coating of snow. Only the skirts of the cloud came over us, however, and we escaped the violence of the storm.

Unfortunately the axle of one of our ambulances (we had two) broke the evening before, and it had been repaired in such a way as to leave some doubts as to its safety for the remainder of the journey. The ladies, therefore, were put into the more serviceable one, and we of the other sex occupied the disabled one. This was rather a quakerish way of dividing up the party; but considering all things, for a fifty-miles' ride, it was thought best, and none of the gentlemen would plead guilty to the charge of want of gallantry.

Our crippled wagon made the journey slow and tedious, and as the sun was getting low, and another storm threatened, the ladies disregarded our injunction not to get far ahead, lest either wagon should meet with an accident, and they hurried on hoping to make Fort Bridger before dark. The storm commenced about sundown, when we were fifteen miles from the post. The whereabouts of the ladies we knew nothing of; but as the night was threatening, we hoped they had stopped at the next ranch. When we reached it we ascertained that they passed about three-quarters of an hour before. It was only twelve miles thence to the Fort, and as they had a good team, and a careful driver, familiar with the road, we hoped that they would make it at an early hour. A consultation was then held as to whether or not we should stop with Mr. Burnes, the owner of the ranch, for the night, or go on to the Fort. Mr. Burnes, we ascertained, had two rooms in his cabin, which were occupied by two families, consisting of about a dozen souls, more or less. We decided to go. The number of necessary bed-fellows, or room-fellows at best, if we remained, may have influenced us somewhat in our decision, and as the storm was increasing we hurried off.

Ascending a hill we were upon a broad plain extending to the Fort. Here the storm was then ten-fold more severe than before, as the bench had protected us. The wind was from the east, and now directly in our faces. The pelting snow in the eyes of the mules made it difficult to keep them in the road, which every minute was becoming more obscure. The curtains of the ambulance broke from their fastenings, and the snow was driven furiously through it, while the night was rapidly growing colder. Our driver soon became so benumbed as to be scarcely able to hold the reins, and it was necessary for one of the party to walk in front of the mules to distinguish the road.

It became evident that the driver must be relieved, or he would freeze, and as Lieutenant S. had had more experience in driving four animals than Mr. Dean or myself, he took the reins, and we wrapped the driver in our only buffalo robe. The mules were jaded, and to get them along required the free application of the whip, which the Lieutenant did not fail to make, together with some expletives which would probably have been omitted if the ladies had been present. In a short time our new driver had to desist, and the original resumed his place, only to relinquish it again in a few minutes, however. About this time Mr. Dean, our pilot, discovered that we were off the road. The storm howled furiously, and so did a pack of hungry wolves that followed us, doubtless expecting that we would soon become their prey. We knew that we were within six miles of the Fort, but we might as well have been sixty, so far as our comfort that night was concerned, for it was evident that we could not reach it. The only thing to be done was to lay up for the night, so we unhitched the mules, and tied them to the leeward of the ambulance. We could make no fire, as we had no wood cut, nor an ax to chop any, and if we had had both, would then have been no better off, for we had no matches. There we were, four of us, on an open plain, in a fearful storm, on a dark night. Our ambulance afforded but little protection — more to the mules on the outside than to those inside—but by lying "spoon-fashion" we all managed to get in, and put the one robe over us. Unfortunately it was not large enough to completely cover the outside parties. Lieutenant S. was one of these, and lay with his back exposed on the side next to the mules. Having had no supper the animals ate the curtains from the ambulance, and next took a piece out of the back of the Lieutenant's overcoat. Mr. Dean was nearly frozen, and he lay so still that we often called him to learn whether he was dead or alive. Being one of the middle ones I suffered less, but spent the night in decidedly unpleasant thoughts. I repeated over and over again "Excelsior," though I felt not the least ambition to emulate the youth's courage in a similar adventure, nor did I very seriously think that I would meet a similar fate. Lieutenant S. was asked the next day by a lady what his thoughts were about, when he replied that he spent the greater part of the night in repeating the Lord's Prayer, which certainly was not in keeping with his audible expressions when he discovered that the mules had eaten a hole in the back of his coat.

After what appeared as an almost interminable night, the day finally dawned, but the storm had abated none of its fury. As soon as it was light enough to see the road, which could be distinguished by the aid of the telegraph poles, we attempted to hitch up the mules, but all were so benumbed as to render it impossible to do so. Then followed another council of war, or council of safety, and it was decided that we would leave the driver, with the robe, which was sufficient to keep one man warm, and the others would walk to the post. Before we had gone three hundred yards Mr. Dean, fearing he would give out, returned to share the robe with the driver. Lieutenant S. and myself pushed forward, wading through snow-drifts three feet deep, and with the wind directly in our faces, driving the snow-flakes against the skin with such force as to sting like the prick of needles.

It seemed a long, long six miles to the post, and more than once the fear was expressed that during the night the wind had turned our ambulance around, and that we were going from the Fort instead of toward it. The falling snow was so thick that no landmarks could be seen, and our minds were not at rest concerning the direction we were pursuing, until we reached one of the branches of Black's-Fork, near the post. It was wide, knee-deep, and running rapidly, but that was no time for hesitation, and we waded it immediately. Before we had walked ten rods further our pants were as stiff as boards from the ice on them. Two other streams were crossed in like manner, and we reached the Fort. We then commenced thawing out; first the ice and snow on my beard, so that I could open my mouth, and then I drank a cup of strong, hot ginger-tea to thaw out my stomach, if in the condition "Uncle Jack" was afraid his would become if he drank water. I then changed all my clothes, giving the body a good rubbing, and after drinking a cup of hot coffee, and eating a hot beefsteak, I was surprised to find myself so comfortable. Until several minutes after I commenced undergoing the process of thawing out, I had not doubted the safe arrival of the ladies in the garrison the night before, and was expecting as soon as I could open my mouth, so as to speak intelligibly, to call upon them and talk over the adventures of the night. The reader can imagine of my surprise and horror, when the husband of one of them rushed into the room where I was, to inquire about his wife, for their ambulance had not arrived. I could reasonably account for their absence in no other way but that they had lost the road and might have wandered far away. A number of soldiers were immediately mounted and sent in all directions (the storm still prevailing) in search of the missing party. An anxious hour to a father, a husband and a brother, as well as to myself, in whose charge the ladies were placed, followed, but they were found and brought safely in. They had come within a mile of the post the night before, when the horses took a road leading from it, and after wandering about for an hour or two, they stopped for the night as we did. Fortunately they had a close ambulance and several robes, and suffered comparatively little from cold, though they imagined that they were so near freezing as to render it dangerous for them to sleep, and they kept awake all night.

A party was sent to the relief of Mr. Dean and the driver, and they too reached the post safely, the former experiencing but little inconvenience; but the driver had his feet and ears so badly frozen as to confine him to the hospital for several weeks.

The thermometer stood at 8° above zero the morning we got in, and I have no idea how it stood during the night, but it was the wind that made the cold so intolerable. I have seen the themometer at the same place indicate 15° below zero when calm, and it did not appear near so cold. The storm was pronounced by old residents the most severe they had ever seen in that locality. I learned a lesson from this trip, and shall never start on a hundred and twenty-five mile journey in this country again without being better provided for protection against cold. It is a good rule to observe in these wild regions, whenever a storm overtakes a traveller, for him to find some protected spot, if possible, stop, build a fire, and wait until the storm ceases. However familiar with the country one may be, he is liable to get lost if he undertakes to travel in a severe snow-storm.

A carriage-ride of one hundred and twenty-five miles in the States, even with comfortable stopping-places for the night, would seem in these days a great undertaking; but after a journey of twelve hundred miles over the plains, and camping out every night for three months, one feels a perfect contempt for distance, and even to the ladies a three-days' ride through the mountains is as a picnic excursion would have been the year before in civilization, nor are the accommodations afforded by the way such as are to be had at the Fifth Avenue. Indeed, we passed but one hotel between the Missouri River and Salt Lake City. Travellers in the Far West discard luxury. If one desires to sleep under a roof, he can be accommodated at any of the stations or ranches; but usually travellers sleep, in or under their wagons except in very severe weather.

As an example of the accommodations to be had, I will describe what was furnished our party on the trip just referred to. We drove one day over fifty miles of the one hundred and twenty-five, to reach a place that was considered a *very desirable* one to stop at over night. We reached the station just at dark, and were tired enough to content ourselves with whatever might offer. I introduced myself to the keeper and made known our wishes, when he promised to do the best he could for us. We soon discovered that the "best," in the way of accommodations, was very limited, and there was not much danger of any ill-feeling growing out of a selection of rooms, for there were but two in the house, a chamber and a room of a very general character. We had all, long before, lost fastidiousness about such things, and made the best of what offered. The ladies were given the chamber, or rather a share with others of their sex already at the station. I have heard of tenement-houses in New York, where several families occupied one large room, and the space allowed for each marked off with chalk on the floor; but on the night referred to, there was not space enough between the pallets for a chalk-mark. Before the last could be spread, the occupants of the room for the night had to collect inside, for there was not space enough left for the door to open.

In the general room adjoining, the gentlemen were allowed the soft side of some cotton-wood boards that composed the floor, together with a few blankets and a buffalo robe, while the proprietor packed himself away in the bed of a wagon back of the house. Fatigue is a most excellent soporific, and in the condition we were half an hour after lying down, so far as comfort was concerned, we may as well have been where we were, as between immaculate linen sheets on a fine hair mattress.

Such is the way travellers fare in a new country; but at

the risk of being tedious on this subject, I will record the experiences of another night out, in the same country. On this occasion I had but one companion, and that a gentleman. It was fortunate that it was so. We were about six or eight miles from our station, travelling in a sleigh, and just at dark our establishment broke down. I meet with such accidents, and lose the road oftener than any other officer in the army. Remembering my experience in a snow-storm, about which I have here told the reader, and there being a prospect of one overtaking us if we started to walk in, we decided to spend the night with an old mountaineer whose cabin was not far away. We led the horses to the place, and of course we were accommodated as we desired, or rather as we could be. This ranch, unfortunately, had but *one* room, in which they cooked, ate, slept, &c. &c. The landlord occupied a bed on a rude bedstead in one corner, and as we entered we discovered several lying around on the dirt floor covered with robes, but as there was no light, except such as was emitted from a few embers on the hearth, we could not distinguish who they were, or how many. The son of the proprietor, whose mother is a squaw, furnished a few dirty robes, and we stretched out in front of the fire, after adding a few sticks which blazed up, and, to some extent, illuminated the room. *I thought* of sleep, but that was as near as I got to it. In a few minutes others commenced dropping in one by one, and soon I found that we were occupying a room with at least a dozen dirty buck Indians, squaws and pappooses. Added to the real discomfort of lying on an uneven piece of ground, were those of my imagination, and a peculiar sensitiveness of my olfactory nerves, and the thoughts of what surrounded me.

We stood it like martyrs until two or three o'clock, when we woke up the proprietor, borrowed a couple of saddles, and started homeward, determined to wander about the country the remainder of the night, if we couldn't find the way, rather than remain.

For about three days, I was constantly smelling smoked

buckskins, Indian paint and Indian filth. A careful examination of my linen, proved that I did leave the cabin *more numerous* than when I entered, which I feared was the case.

CHAPTER X.

FROM FORT BRIDGER TO WANSHIP SETTLEMENT.

At Fort Bridger we left two other companies, which reduced our column to a very small remnant of the large command that left Fort Leavenworth.

Only three companies remained, and these were destined for Camp Douglas, where our long but pleasant march was to terminate. Two ladies also left us here—Mrs. Major Burt, whose husband was to assume command, and Miss Reynolds, her sister. These ladies had been universally esteemed, and their society highly prized. Mrs. Burt was regarded by every one as an example of what an army officer's wife should be.

Directly west of the post is an elevation of peculiar appearance, known as Bridger's Butte, and also as the Flat Mountain. It is a piece of table-land, its surface several square miles in extent, and as flat and smooth as the country between New Orleans and Lake Ponchartrain, and of an elevation of several hundred feet above the fort. The ascent to it appeared easy, but I found considerable difficulty in making it, though the prospect afforded from so elevated a position well repaid me for the trouble. The entire valley, with all the bench-lands, and the mountains surrounding these, many miles away, could be taken in at a glance.

It was the most extended view I ever had, and the beauty of the landscape was hardly surpassed by the prospect afforded from the Black Hills which I endeavored to describe in a previous letter. To the south and east, was the long range of Uintah Mountains, and far to the west rose the majestic Wasach. Through the valley could be traced the courses of the streams, by the growth of small trees upon their banks, and off in the direction of the Uintahs was the large forest of pines, cedars and cotton-wood, to which I have before referred. When beholding such scenes I would wish for a moment for the genius of the painter or the poet, but I would soon after thank God that I was not a genius in any profession.

A few miles further west we come to the Little and Big Muddy streams—very inappropriately named for brooks running over pebbly beds with water as clear as a crystal. At other seasons, and perhaps in other places at the same season, the water is not so clear, and as they were probably first seen by the old mountaineer Bridger when muddy, their classic misnomer will ever attach to them.

Not far from the Muddies there is a mineral spring, the waters of which is strongly impregnated with magnesium, and contains also other mineral properties, and is of a very low temperature. There we encamped for the night. The next day our journey lay over a more uneven country, and we passed Quaking-asp Hill, the highest elevation crossed by the stage-road between the Missouri River and Salt Lake, and I am told has an altitude of more than eight thousand feet. The hill derives its name from a species of poplar which grows on the summit, the leaves of which have a constant tremulous motion in the wind. From the brow of the hill there is considerable descent, within the distance of a mile, and thence onward we found a succession of hills and mountains, either to be crossed in our journey or contiguous to the road. Beyond Quaking-asp the next sight that attracted my attention was that of the worm fences and cultivated fields on Bear River. I had seen nothing of the kind west of Kansas, and I was carried back in my recollection to the farms of old Virginia and Maryland, and was led to a contemplation of the undeveloped agricultural resources of the great western country over which we had marched, much of which could be made to yield as abundantly as the farms in the valley of the Shenandoah or the fields in the valley before me.

On our march we have crossed streams that flow into the Gulf of Mexico, others that send their waters to the Pacific, and now we cross one that might be said to empty into the clouds. Perhaps they all might, but this particularly, as it flows into the Great Salt Lake, where there is no outlet, and where the evaporation is so rapid that the water disappears about as fast as it enters.

Not many miles beyond Bear River, I observed in the side and near the top of a tall hill an opening, which proved to be Cache Cave, a place long familiar to the mountaineer of this region, and which had often afforded shelter to the passing emigrant and hunter during the fearful storms which so often prevail in this mountainous country during the winter. I rode to the mouth and, dismounting, entered and found the cave to measure about thirty-five feet each way, and eight feet high in the centre. The names of hundreds of visitors were cut in the soft sandstone in which the cave is formed, and I noticed among them a Clara— and a Jennie—, but I will give no further publicity to the fair fame-seekers. It seemed an anomaly in the order of things to find the names of the gentler sex in this wild region, associated with those of the rough and hardy of the other gender.

Such a continuation of wild and grand scenery as had been afforded on the march from Bridger I had not witnessed on any previous part of our journey, and what yet awaits my description, before entering Salt Lake Valley, so increases in grandeur and sublimity that I shrink from the task of attempting it. Descriptions from far abler pens than my own, have fallen far short of my appreciations of the scenes when I beheld them, that I feel inclined to leave the reader at the head of Echo Cañon, and have him join me again in the vicinity of the Mormon's "Zion," when I might say something about the works of art, and leave the awful grandeur of nature as seen in some parts of the route I passed over not further alluded to, hoping that he may at some future time have an opportunity to see what I saw, but am unable to describe. However, we must glance at some of the salient points as we pass along.

Descending a somewhat steep hill we entered a valley, the head of Echo Cañon, which runs thence to the Weber River, a distance of a little more than twenty miles. On either side the land rises by gentle slopes (but here and there more abruptly) into high hills; and as we proceeded down it, the graceful declivities on the northern side gradually disappeared, and perpendicular bluffs of a conglomerate of red clay and pebbles, from four hundred to six hundred feet high, were found instead. At the commencement the cañon is nearly a mile wide, but its width gradually lessens until it becomes almost a gorge; and on the south the hills, which continue sloping on their surface, become steeper and taller.

This cañon is the great highway through the mountains to Salt Lake Valley, and it was here, about its narrow gorges, that the Mormon army was stationed in '57, to prevent the onward march of General Johnston to "Zion." Their position was on the north side of the cañon, and on the tall bluffs they erected their rifle-pits, and at the most precipitous points immense boulders were placed, in such positions as to be easily rolled upon the heads of those who might attempt to pass below. They also constructed dams across the pass, down which flows a stream so as to flood it to a considerable depth. Some of the breast works and dams still remain. While the precautions thus taken would have effectually prevented the onward march of a body of troops along the road, the position of the Saint army was an entirely untenable one. A body of infantry from the hills on the south, which perfectly commanded the rude works, and to the possession of which no obstacles were thrown in the way, could in a short time have dislodged the enemy. But it will be remembered that no fighting occurred, and had our forces approached within threatening distance, the Prophet would doubtless have had a vision in the night and moved his deluded followers to a place of greater security.

The only casualty among the Mormons, that I know of, during their short campaign in the cañon, was the killing of a saint by one of his comrades, under the following circumstances. The man stood upon a tall cliff, and shouted to his companions below to shoot him if they could. It is more difficult to correctly estimate a distance perpendicularly than horizontally, and the man on the bluff thought he was beyond range, and so did the man who shot at him, in all probability, but the ball took effect and killed him on the spot.

Passing this part of the cañon amidst the shouts of the soldiers, for the reverberating effect, we soon came near its mouth, where we encamped. Opposite our tents the bluffs and hills were as high as elsewhere, and during the afternoon some of the soldiers climbed to the highest points and shouted jocularly to their comrades below about the appearance of Trinity Church spire and the Astor House, from their elevated stand-point.

The name of the cañon is well taken. The echo along the lower part of it where the bluffs are highest is loud and perfect, and where we encamped the most remarkable effect followed the beating of drums and the sounding of bugles. With the former all was confusion of sounds, and with the latter, when the short notes were sounded, not much more harmony existed; but when the bugle calls were long and slow the perfect repetition of each note in the echo was heard with fine effect. But I failed to appreciate any beauty in the call for tents to be struck on the morning of our departure. All the luxuries, in the way of diet, with which I started from Leavenworth, had been consumed, and a few weeks before signs of scurvy appearing among the men, the officers had turned over to those affected the last of their potatoes—the only fresh vegetables then remaining. Our bill of fare had consequently become rather curtailed as to variety; but in the vicinity I obtained lettuce, onions, radishes, new potatoes, eggs, butter, &c., and the morning referred to my cook prepared a breakfast of broiled trout, boiled eggs, fried potatoes, radishes, hot cakes fit for royalty, and when in the midst of it, the loud and familiar sound of the bugle and its reverberations told that the tents must fall. Would the reader have been less disgusted than I was? But I finished my breakfast as they lifted the tent over me. Afterward, when mounted on my horse and leisurely smoking my pipe, I better enjoyed the effect of the echo to the call to which the soldiers have applied the words:

> "I know you are tired, but still you must go,
> So shoulder your musket and march along slow."

On the trip to Fort Bridger, that terminated in an adventure in a snow-storm, to which I referred in my last, I was much amused by a teamster we met in this cañon. Coming to a miry place, our ambulances were halted for me to select the best crossing, and at the same time a rather Hoosier-like fellow, with two or three wagons, approached the opposite side of the slough. I had about decided where to attempt the crossing when he came up, but thinking I might profit by his larger experience, we had a conversation as follows:

"This is rather a bad place, sir," said I.

"Well—yes—'tis a little damp." (We afterward found the liquid mud to be a foot and a half deep.)

"But don't you think it safer to attempt to cross here than above?"

"Well—yes—you might try."

"Do you think it safe to make the attempt with the ladies in the ambulance?"

"Well—yes—don't see any mules' ears, or wagon bows sticking out—somebody has crossed, or gone clean under."

"Seriously, don't you think there is a firm bottom under this mud?"

"Well—yes—if you go down deep enough to reach it."

"Joking aside, my friend, would you advise me to attempt it here or at the crossing above?"

"Well—don't know—this is narrow, and if you go under here, then you know exactly where your wagon has gone down."

"I see I can't get much out of you—Do you intend to cross here?"

"You bet."

There was more in the fellow's manner and tone of voice that was amusing, than in what he said, and he caused one of the ladies to laugh away a headache. We crossed without difficulty, but when our laconic stranger attempted it, in the same place, his loaded wagons sank deep, and the first stuck fast, when we had a good laugh at his expense, while he was doubling teams to pull it out.

On the Weber I beheld still more familiar and more beautiful sights than I observed on Bear River. In addition to fields of wheat, barley and oats which grew in great luxuriance, the vegetable gardens at the station-house were filled with all the table vegetables cultivated in the same, and more southern latitudes in the States. The green lettuce and the onion-tops appeared more beautiful as they grew there because of the contrast with the wild rugged hills and bluffs close by, and the hills and bluffs appeared more wild and sublime because of the contrast with the tender cultivated plants at their base.

The Weber is a stream abounding with trout, and some of them larger than in the streams near Fort Bridger, to which I referred in my last. Though we are supposed to have started on the march I must tell the reader of my trout-fishing the day before. It was in the Weber where I indulged in that sport for the first time in my life—others of the command had caught them in several places further east.

I had heard of trout-fishing from early boyhood, but had never before been in a country where they are caught, and I longed to indulge in the sport. So during the afternoon we were in camp near the stream I prepared my tackle and went alone to try my luck. I had scarcely got my line into the water when it was grabbed with all the dash which characterizes the bite of the trout, and with a jerk as quick I threw the speckled beauty on the bank. It was an epoch in my life! I had caught my first trout! And I was as delighted as a little girl with her first doll on a Christmas morning. Subsequent to this event I have indulged freely in the sport, and on one occasion I knew of fifty-four being caught in a few hours by one individual.

The station at the mouth of the cañon is kept by a Mormon, and several of the same faith live in the vicinity. My first impressions of them for thrift and industry were favorable. I purchased vegetables of a "Saint," who is "the husband of one wife" (not *at least* one, as they explain St. Paul's injunction to mean), or rather I purchased them of the wife who appeared to be the better *man* of the two; and I would here add that this is the only instance I have observed in my intercourse with Mormons where the woman was treated as if she had any rights whatever, or her judgment and opinion respected in the least. But of the Mormons more hereafter.

Around the stage stations, everywhere from Atchison to Salt Lake City, large flocks of the common blackbirds were constantly collected; but at the mouth of Echo Cañon I saw for the first time those of the magpie species. They are larger than the common blackbird in the States, with a larger tail, in which white feathers predominate, and parts of their wings are of the same. The white feathers looked whiter and the black blacker because of the association of the two. It is too pretty a bird for one of its habits, which are the same as the crow's. Ravens are very numerous in this country, also; but the reader must not suppose that the ravens of the Rocky Mountain regions, and the crows that are such a nuisance to the farmers in Virginia, and elsewhere in the South, are the same bird. Of course they belong to the same family; but the former are larger, have a broader and stouter bill, and are of a more glossy black, nor do they make quite such unmusical sounds, or so many of them, as the crows. The above, with a few turtle-doves, were the only things of the bird kind in this section of country, so the guns were packed away, and fishing rods and lines took their places.

The Weber River, along which our route lay for several miles, flows into the Dead Sea of America a short distance below the mouth of the Bear River. Along this stream there are numerous farms, and nearly the whole country, as far as we marched, was cut up by fences. The farms here are irrigated from streams that flow into the river. The stream down Echo, Chalk creek, a few miles south of it, and other mountain streams, are made useful in this way. The grain fields were just ripening for harvest when we passed, and in this valley wheat, oats and rye yield almost as luxuriantly as in the most fertile parts of the valley of the Great Salt Lake, of which I shall say something in a future letter.

Passing southward we soon came to a settlement of the followers of Brigham, known as Coalville, and so named because of the coal found there, and is the source from which Salt Lake City is supplied with that fuel. It requires to be hauled fifty miles.

Coalville contains about seventy-five small houses, and has a population of about five hundred, including children, who largely predominate. Most of the houses are of logs, very roughly constructed, but there are also several neat adobe residences and stores. I was pleased with the appearance of one of the buildings, and approaching I read on a slab over the door, "Coalville Meeting-house." I felt disposed to respect the deluded people for setting apart the best house in their village as a place of worship; but when passing through the place, on another occasion, I observed hanging by the side of the door of their "Meeting-house" a variety of specimens of the art of the photographer. Whether or not the house had been converted into a photographic establishment as a more profitable use to put it to, or the artist and priest used it jointly, I am unable to say, but am inclined to the opinion that the minister was also the photographer, and had combined his spiritual and secular interest in an economical way.

A few miles below Coalville we passed another Mormon settlement of more recent origin, the name of which I did not learn. From Echo Cañon to this point the land along the river is fenced in, though but little of it is cultivated. Crossing the river we marched to at hird settlement, called Wanship.

CHAPTER XI.

FROM WANSHIP TO SALT LAKE VALLEY.

WANSHIP is a Mormon village of about three hundred inhabitants, and is located on the overland stage route, near the Weber River. It consists of houses along both sides of the road, and the gardens attached to each, like in most country villages, causes it to stretch out to a considerable length.

A German has here established a lager beer brewery for the accommodation of travellers whose Tuetonic tastes lead them to indulge in this drink, which, by the way, is fast becoming a national one in this country. I took a glass or two, and I think I must have done so simply because it is called by the same name as the good beer in St. Louis, of which I was so fond—certainly not because I relished the poor stuff.

Near the upper end of the village I stopped at the house of one of the settlers, whose garden presented a fine appearance, to replenish my stock of vegetables for the remainder of the journey. I was received by a stout English woman who treated me courteously, and signified her willingness to accommodate me with a portion of anything the garden produced. She called for "Sister," when a much rougher looking Danish woman appeared and accompanied me to the garden to gather the vegetables. I afterward learned that the "Sister" was also the wife of her husband, and I was for the first time under the roof of a polygamist. Both lived in the same house, but their duties appeared to be very distinct. The English woman appeared to be the Mary of the household, and the Dane the Martha. I had no account of their conjugal history, but am very much inclined to think that the former was the last espoused. The Dane appeared more like a woman hired to work in the garden, and her labor was certainly worth more than the cost of her subsistence and clothing. The vegetables being ready I asked the bill, when the Dane looked as if she was somewhat doubtful as to the capacity of my pocket-book, and hesitated, but the "Sister" thought it had better be left to the gentleman to pay what he pleased. I insisted on the amount being named, and then appreciated the diplomacy of the liberal (?) party, for I should have never offered so small a sum. After drinking a glass of buttermilk I started, and as we did so the English "Sister" expressed the hope that an officer who was with me might have his eyes opened and become a bright shining light in the Church of Latter Day Saints—"and who knows but such may be the case!" said she. In my conversation she seemed to feel no interest. She appeared to be the happiest duplicate wife I ever saw. Her Danish colleague was by no means so jovial, and though she appeared resigned to her fate, looked by no means contented or happy.

Running by the village on to the Weber River, where it empties, is a clear, beautiful stream, fitly named Silver Creek, and but a short distance above we entered the mouth of a cañon through which the stream flows, and from it the cañon takes its name. It was narrow from the first, and the tall hills on either side rose to a greater altitude than those along Echo Cañon, to which I referred in my last, but they are nowhere abrupt and precipitate. The base of the hills ran almost to the banks of the stream; the road was cut in the slope on the western side, and in order to make it wide enough for a single wagon, in some places it was necessary to cut a perpendicular bank of ten or twelve feet. The dashing mail-coach is the terror of those who drive light vehicles along these narrow places. Throughout the cañon the range of tall hills on both sides was quite destitute of gorges or abrupt cliffs, and many with neatly rounded dome-like summits. The cañon being so narrow, where there was a somewhat short curve in its course the hills on the two sides appeared to meet and terminate the pass, and more than once was I completely deceived, thinking it impossible to go much further without ascending a very steep hill, but I looked in vain for the road up its sides, and going to the spot, found it to continue on as before, only changing its direction. The windings of the cañon added to the beauty of the scenery. But the most attractive feature was the beautiful creek. Along it, and it was constantly in sight, the green leaves of the willow, and the shrubbery growing on its banks, contrasted beautifully with the silvery waters that glided by them, and a more lovely sight of this character I never beheld. In places the water ran over pebbles and boulders, which could be seen as distinctly as if through the clearest crystal, and here and there a little cascade leaped from a projecting rock to form an eddy below, so inviting as a lurking-place for the mountain trout. And gushing from the hill by the roadside were numerous springs, rivalling, if possible, the clear waters of the creek. Amid such beauties of nature we marched about eight miles. It was the season best suited for seeing the cañon with its greatest attractions. All nature seemed to conspire to render the scene grand and lovely!

Leaving the cañon we passed over a ridge to Parley's Park, a wide valley or basin, nearly surrounded by mountains and hills. It might be easily irrigated, and the whole might be put under a high degree of cultivation, provided the climate is not too cold, for like Fort Bridger this locality is very high. This park, as well as the cañon, which we will reach presently, are named after a prominent Mormon, Parley Pratt, once one of the Apostles, who was assassinated a few years ago by the enraged husband of a woman who became a convict to Mormonism, through the ministry of

Pratt in California, and afterward joined him as his fifth wife.

In this basin, Mr. Kimball, a son of Heber C. Kimball, the second President of the Church, has erected the largest and best built house I had seen west of the magnificent mansion of Mr. Majors, near Atchison, Kansas. It is of stone, two stories, with a long back building, and is used as a hotel. Mr. Kimball is a Mormon, having three wives, one of whom lives with him at the hotel, a second occupies a rude log cabin on the opposite side of the road, and the third is at his residence in the city.

Mr. Kimball in his conversation with me appeared to be the most reasonable and liberal man of that faith with whom I have conversed. At one time he was a prominent Elder in the church, and has been missionary in England, but latterly takes little interest in her affairs. He has a large inclosed and cultivated farm, and raises herds of sheep and cattle, which graze upon the mountains and the lowlands around his premises. In many parts of Utah there are fine grazing lands, and though I may not have seen "cattle upon a thousand hills," I think I have seen there a thousand cattle upon a hill. Were it not for the hostility of the Indians I imagine the territory would raise more stock than at present. The resident Indians of Utah have been hostile to the Mormons, but I think are so because it is profitable to be, and not because of any unfair dealing with them, as they charge upon the settlers. I am of the opinion that a population of Gentiles would be subjected to exactly the same annoyances and depredations. I have not the slightest confidence in the Indians, and will give my reasons for not having in a future letter.

In the valley a short distance from Mr. Kimball's, another settlement is about starting, and a few miles west of that we crossed a tall ridge of the Wasach Mountains, known as "The Summit," and soon commenced to descend through Parley's Cañon. For six miles the scenery is not unlike that in parts of Silver Creek Cañon, but here the eminences may be called mountains, and in the other, hills; but in the lower portion the scenery is more wild and romantic.

The feelings of admiration for the beautiful in nature as seen in my ride along Silver Creek, watching its "laughing waters," were changed to those of wonder and awe, when I stood before the towering mountains and rugged cliffs in Parley's Cañon. There nature was seen in her wildest and most majestic forms. Great strata of rocks, hundreds of feet thick, as they lay where originally formed, had been fissured through, and on one side of the fissure thrown up to form immense mountains bordering the cañon. The strata of these were as regular as when they were subterranean horizontal layers; but now running at an angle of forty-five degrees, and where they had broken off, cropped out along the sides of almost perpendicular bluffs. In places they could be seen only along the one side where they terminated; but here and there a mass had been thrown up, which had been fissured in two ways where the strata could be traced along its sides also. The thought of the force required thus to upheave the very foundations of the earth was an almost overwhelming thought. It filled me with profound awe and reverence. The terrific force still pent up in the bowels of the earth beneath, I could never before so fully comprehend as when I observed its effects there before me. Had I known nothing of the Creator I should have worshipped the "Unknown God," amid such wonderful evidences of majestic power.

The cañon varies much in width and in some places the stream runs so near the bluffs as not to permit two wagons to pass. In such places many teams had to wait for our column and train to get by, and even the mail-coach had to give up the right of way.

The stream here is larger than Silver Creek, and its fall in twelve or fifteen miles I would estimate as considerably over two thousand feet; and as there are no cascades of more than a few feet in height, the water along the cañon rushes rapidly over its uneven and rocky bed. A curious and beautiful phenomenon appeared on the slope of the mountain on the south side as we were nearing the terminus of the pass. It was a large stream pouring from an opening in the grouud·about half-way between summit and base, and forming a torrent along the mountain side to the stream in the valley below. It was doubtless a drain from mountains south, which after making a subterranean passage through the range bordering the cañon gushed out from its hiding-place where I saw it. If a view of Harper's Ferry on the Potomac is worth a trip from Europe, as Mr. Jefferson represented it was, certainly a sight of Echo and Parley's cañons is worth a continuation of the journey through the Rocky Mountains.

We camped for a night amid some of these scenes, and again, for the last time on our journey, I indulged in the sport of trout-fishing. On the Weber River I could wait in one place for the trout to come along, but in the smaller mountain streams they waited for me, and I had to find their rambling places, requiring much more exertion, but the sport amply repaid. In one hole, a few feet from my tent, I caught several, but I walked two miles before abandoning the sport.

As we approached the terminus of this, the last pass of our journey, the mountains separated wider, and more of the clear blue sky could be seen in front of us. Leaving the road to the city, we took another winding around the mountain side, and before emerging entirely from the cañon we came to another lager beer brewery, but satisfied with my experience at the last, and being impatient to reach a position but a little beyond, from which I could view the great valley, I passed without stopping.

But here I must leave the reader, and in my next will attempt to describe the scene beyond, which is to the Mormon emigrant, after his long and toilsome journey, a source of delight almost as great as was the sight of the cross to Bunyan's Christian.

CHAPTER XII.

SALT LAKE VALLEY AND THE CITY.

WINDING around the side of the mountain from the lager beer brewery, we were soon upon a bench beyond the range, with the rich valley of the Great Salt Lake stretched out before us. It was a clear, pleasant morning—not a cloud in the sky, and everything conspiring to make the prospect enjoyable. The interests of our command all centred in Camp Douglas, and the eyes of officers and soldiers instinctively turned to the north, and gazed upon their new home with a delight almost equal to that of the Mormon proselyte, when, after the same journey, and from the same stand-point, he beholds for the first time his new Zion.

Camp Douglas is situated upon the tallest of a series of benches which rise one above another from the valley to the base of the mountains on the east. Its white buildings, surrounding a tall staff, from which the stars and stripes floated to the breeze, was a pretty sight; but there was too much to be seen for this to occupy my attention more than a few moments.

Immediately below the post, to the west, lay the renowned Salt Lake City. In the distance it appeared like a large nursery; its fruit-trees almost obscuring the smaller houses, which they everywhere surrounded. Here and there a larger building rose above the green foliage, and the immense arch of the unfinished tabernacle was conspicuous beyond the rest. North of the city was the lake formed by the waters of the hot springs, and west, the Great Salt Lake, with its mountain islands rising from the water. Near its southeastern border commenced the West Mountains, which run south to near Utah Lake—the most southerly part of the valley visible from my stand-point, though it extends far beyond; thence, along the eastern border of the valley, rose the majestic Wasach Mountains, through which we had passed, and towering up, almost above us, were the "Twin Peaks," their snow-crowned summits in remarkable contrast with the green fields of the valley and the fruit-trees of the city.

Through the valley flowed the waters of Jordan from Utah Lake to the Dead Sea, and along its banks the fields of grain, just ripening for the harvest, dotted the surface of the plain before me. Beyond the river the deposits of alkali, shining under the sun's rays, looked like miniature lakes. But no description of mine will lead to a proper appreciation of the beauty of this landscape scene. And all this valley, twenty years ago, was a wild, sterile waste, which, by the persevering industry of the laborious Mormon, has been made to "blossom like the rose." Where formerly only sage-brush and grease-wood grew, and the mountaineer thought it would be madness to attempt to cultivate, there are now fields of wheat, oats and barley, yielding an average of forty bushels to the acre, while the more fertile and better cultivated farms sometimes produce eighty and ninety.

When the emigrant Mormons first entered the valley with a view to cultivating it, the old settlers in the vicinity said they would give them a hundred dollars for every bushel of grain they raised them. If the mountaineers had made good their offer the Mormons would now be an immensely wealthy people. They have certainly wrought a great change in the country. I award to them all credit for their enterprise and industry.

Camp Douglas was established in 1862, by the then Col. Patrick E. Connor, of the Third California Volunteer Infantry, which regiment arrived in the valley in the fall of that year. Temporary quarters were built for the troops the first winter, and the following summer the present post was erected. Col. Connor was afterward made brigadier-general, and assigned to the command of the district of Utah, when he established his headquarters at this post. The garrison is built of wood, with quarters for eight companies. The troops occupying them upon our arrival belonged to California and Nevada volunteer regiments, under the command of Lieutenant-Colonel Johns, who appeared to be a good officer, and was not lacking in the amenities which should pertain to his position, as commanding officer, upon the arrival of a new command.

The post was in a very good condition compared with the one we last visited (Bridger), and since our arrival has not only been greatly improved in general appearance, but Major Grimes, the Quartermaster, has added some very large store-rooms, and stables.

But I have something to write about of more interest to the reader than a detailed description of Camp Douglas, and will occupy no more space with that now.

We reached there about noon, and after dining with the hospitable surgeon, Dr. Hamilton, I immediately started on a tour of observation. Cleanliness being ranked by some very high in the catalogue of virtues, I first resorted to the warm sulphur springs, and took a bath, thus combining a gratification of curiosity with utility. There are several of these near together, two miles north of the city. The water from the largest is conducted to a house containing a tank or reservoir, eighteen by twenty feet, and about five feet deep. The stream, almost large enough to turn a mill, enters the tank on one side, and an opening on the opposite side prevents it from overflowing, and it is thus kept constantly supplied with fresh water as it runs from the spring in the hill-side. In the centre, above the warm water, is a platform, with a cold shower-bath over it, very suggestive of shocks to the nervous system. Near the plunge-bath is a larger building, conveniently fitted up with bathing-tubs, after the manner of the better class of bath-houses in our eastern cities. This part of the establishment is supplied with water of the same temperature, and is for the accommodation of both ladies and gentlemen. I chose the plunge-bath, and plunging in, experienced a sensation near akin to that of scalding; but in a minute the temperature was endurable and even pleasant. Remaining immersed too long, however, I paid the penalty in the enervation that followed. The water is soft and delightful for a bath, is strongly impregnated with sulphur, which gives it a light blue color, and I should judge the temperature to be above one hundred degrees.

Salt Lake City is on the lowest bench of land between the Jordan and the mountains on the east. The site is well selected, with a view to drainage and irrigation, and altogether it has a very desirable location. It could be enlarged almost indefinitely with the same advantages as a city it now possesses.

Washington must surrender to Salt Lake City the expressive name given to it by John Randolph, and no longer be called the "City of Magnificent Distances."

Salt Lake City is regularly laid out, with the streets at right angles. The squares are of uniform size, containing, as originally planned, eight lots of one and a quarter acres each. Many of these have been divided and subdivided, and on the business streets cut up into building lots.

In the early part of its existence there was built along the north and south boundaries of the city, a tall wall of earth, nominally for defence against the Indians, but really to afford labor to the suffering and disaffected Saints. The chosen people of God, as they claim to be, in these latter days were not exempt from the infirmities that characterized God's chosen people of old. As they murmured against Moses, when suffering in a desolate country, so the Latter Day Saints murmured against Brigham for bringing them out to die in the wilderness, as they thought.

There was trouble then in Zion, that threatened serious consequences to the new church, but Brigham Young was equal to the emergency. He would not allow them to live in idleness, and think over their misfortunes, so he encouraged all kinds of amusements, and employed large numbers to build this wall, which was really of no utility; and when the necessity for finding employment in this way for the people had passed, the work was stopped, and the defences of the city were not completed. We cannot now "walk about Zion and consider her bulwarks," for even those that once existed have been allowed to crumble, and wash away, and only fragments remain to mark the places where the defences were once building.

The large majority of the houses in Salt Lake City are small, one-story frame or adobe tenements, but there are many handsome residences and fine stores. The latter are built of red sandstone, obtained in the vicinity, or of adobes, plastered and painted in imitation of masonry. There are residences in Salt Lake City that would attract attention, from their fine appearance, in the western district of New Orleans, and the store of Mr. Jennings, a Mormon merchant, would be creditable to Canal street. A very large proportion of the houses, off the business streets, are surrounded by gardens, varying in size from the original lots to a quarter of an acre, and in these grow fruit-trees of several varieties, often entirely surrounding the houses, which, except on Main street, are required to be set back several feet from the front line of the lot. Almost every family raises its own table vegetables, and the market is supplied with all kinds of fruit and berries, in season, from the gardens within the city limits.

But little rain falls in Salt Lake City, or indeed anywhere in the valley, hence it is necessary to secure moisture for vegetation in some other way. This is done by irrigation. The gardens in the city are watered by streams from the mountains, to the east and northeast, which are so conducted as to run along the streets. The ditches cut for these streams make it as unpleasant to drive through the streets of Salt Lake City, as in the national capital, where they are about as badly cut up with uncovered gutters. Little drains are dug leading into all the gardens, and water conducted to them according to the demands of the things cultivated. For this irrigating water the property-holder is charged just as he would be for Croton water on his premises in New York. The supply as at present conducted to the city would not be equal to the demand, if the water ran through all the gardens at the same time, which indeed is unnecessary, so it is furnished to a certain number for certain specified hours, and is then shut off from these to supply others.

Taking the city as a whole, it presents more the appearance of a New England village, or the suburbs of a southern town, save in the style of its buildings.

The curiosity of the visitor naturally leads him to see, first, the President's Block and Temple Square. The former, on South Temple street, fronting south, is surrounded by a ten-foot wall of cobble-stones, set in cement. On the southwest corner is a large building, where the "*Deseret News*" is printed, and adjoining is a row of one-story buildings, where a few favored ones are allowed to live within the inclosure. Next comes the "Lion House," a long two-story building, gable end to the street, with the representation of a lion, cut in stone, nearly life-size, over the entrance. This is the Prophet's harem, where the majority of his wives reside. Whether or not the lion over the entrance is indicative of the ferocity that would be visited upon the head of a Gentile who dare enter there, I am unable to say. Next beyond is the Bee-Hive House, so named from a representation of a hive that surmounts the centre of the roof, which is the Prophet's own residence, and adjoining is his business sanctum, and the general business office of the Church. Between the Lion House and the Bee-Hive House, is a large gate-way which is the entrance to City Creek Cañon, and over this is the figure of an eagle. City Creek Canon has been conveyed to Brigham Young by an act of the territorial legislature, notwithstanding it is unsurveyed Government land. In this cañon is all the wood to be had in the vicinity of the city, and the Prophet requires one load in every three that are cut for the privilege of collecting fuel on his property.

Last in the row of houses, and a little further removed, stands the residence of the "first wife," who lives in great seclusion, and is but seldom seen by any one, Mormon or

Gentile. The tithing offices, where tithes are paid in produce, is on the side of the square facing west, and is a long row of one-story buildings. In rear of Mr. Young's residence is the church store, where the faithful may purchase on credit what they require, and pay for it in produce or otherwise, as best suits their convenience, when rendering the yearly account of their stewardship. There is also a school-house in the inclosure, where the younger Youngs' young ideas are taught to shoot.

Within the inclosure which surrounds all these buildings, and takes in a number of acres, grow some of the choicest variety of the peach, pear and apple. These fruit are excellent, and so are the strawberries and raspberries, which are also largely cultivated in the city; but the grape has not reached that degree of excellence that characterizes the others.

Most of these buildings, when erected, were palaces compared to others in Zion, (particularly the Lion House, which is said to have cost $65,000), and for neatness and solid substantial appearance, they are ahead of the more recently constructed residences of other dignitaries in the church, some of which present a very fine appearance. Some of the Mrs. Youngs, I am told, live without the defences of their husband, and occupy private residences in other parts of the city.

Temple Square is next west of that in which the Prophet resides, Main street running between. It is to contain the Temple and Tabernacle. The former has been fifteen years' building, and is now only a few feet above ground. The plan of the building makes it to be one hundred and eighty-six and a half feet long, from east to west, and ninety-nine feet from north to south. There are to be towers on the four corners, and centre towers, also, a little taller than the others, on the east and west ends, all of which project but slightly above the roof, and are to be one hundred and ninety and two hundred feet high.

Cuts of the Temple as it is to be, or rather as it is planned to be, make it a massive, substantial-looking edifice. It

TABERNACLE. SALT LAKE CITY.

combines several kinds of architecture, though the combination is well made, and does not destroy the beauty of the building. The work on the Temple is progressing with a view to its greater durability than the one destroyed at Nauvoo, Illinois. The blocks of granite of which the foundation is made, are not only dressed on the face, but the six sides of the cubes are made as regular and even as the square and spirit-level of the mechanic can make them. The masonry now in, unless disturbed by man or nature, in other ways than the ordinary changes wrought by time, will exist for thousands of years.

But it is the universal opinion with anti-Mormons, and I have no doubt with many observing ones of the Faith, also, that the Temple will be longer in building than Solomon's was, or in other words, that it will never be completed. A very small number of workmen are now employed on it—just sufficient to make it appear that the work is progressing, and afford an excuse for collecting to prosecute it. Many have already secured seats in the Temple by contributing funds for that special purpose. A story is told of a saint who lived in a remote part of the territory, and had paid for a choice seat, who visited Zion, and expected to occupy her place in the Temple, thinking the structure actually existed as represented in lithographs she had seen.

There is a little incident connected with building the Temple which I must mention here. The stone of which the structure is to be reared is brought from the mountains, a number of miles distant, and to facilitate its transportation, the Prophet had a canal cut from the quarry toward the city; but a blunder of the engineer ruined the enterprise. The end of the canal in the city was unfortunately higher than where it started from the quarry, and while Mr. Young could not "remove mountains," neither was his faith sufficient to overcome another natural law, and make water run up hill.

The Tabernacle is in the same inclosure, and is to consist of an immense wooden arch, supported on stone pilasters, ten on twelve feet high. The span of the arch is one hundred and eighty feet, and its length two hundred and fifty feet, with ends rounded off, and to rest on similar supports at the sides. It is to be used as a place of worship in the summer season only, and below the arch is to be left open. The Prophet informed me, and I have no doubt he is good authority in such matters, that the arch of the Tabernacle has a wider span than any other wooden arch in the world. It is calculated to seat twelve thousand persons. It is progressing rapidly toward completion, and nearly the whole arch now is covered in.

An immense organ is also building, and I have no doubt within a year the new Tabernacle will be occupied.

The present Tabernacle, which is in the same inclosure, consists of a long, low, shed-like building, capable of seating less than a thousand people, and is used only in the winter. During the warm season their worship is in the "Bowery." This consists of a shelter from the sun, made of green boughs placed on a frame-work of timber, about ten feet above the ground. At one end is the pulpit, of very large size, made of rough boards, which are whitewashed. Along the back of this are arranged the seats for the officials, a host of whom occupy the pulpit whenever there is public service. The President's seat is in the middle, and extending from, toward either end of the row; the other officials, of whom I shall speak in another letter, are seated according to rank—the highest next to Brigham's colleagues in the presidency, who are seated on his right and left. Sunday afternoon service in the Bowery reminded me very much of old-fashioned camp-meetings I sometimes attended when a boy.

Next to the Bowery the theatre is the most popular place for the faithful in Zion. It is always filled when there is a play, and by a class of people certainly not capable of a very profound appreciation of the drama. They probably go from a sense of duty (the same that takes them to the Bowery on the Sabbath), for the theatre is owned by the President, and conducted by one of his sons-in-law for his father-in-law's pecuniary benefit. Every saint then that pays his entrance fee, considers that he is keeping Brother Brigham, and to do so is to him a pleasure.

The theatre is the largest building in the city. It has a very plain exterior, but I am informed that the interior arrangement cannot be surpassed for completeness and elegance by any theatre in the country, since the burning of the Academy of Music in New York city. Near the theatre is the City Hall, one of the finest buildings in the city. It is built of red sandstone, and the tin covering of the rounded top of its cupola on the centre of the roof, is conspicuous from all the approaches to the city In another part of the city is a somewhat similar building, the court-house of the "State of Deseret."

The public hall of the "Council of Seventy," is in the same locality, and so is the "Social Hall," belonging to Brigham, which is hired for balls, &c. There is but one hotel in the city, the Salt Lake House, which is a two-story building, with limited accommodations, often insufficient for the demand, and would not be creditable to any town of five thousand inhabitants east of the Mississippi.*

The hotel, like the theatre, I have been told by good authority, is the property of Brigham Young, and is conducted for him by a relative. A skeptic might suppose that the President has some regard for lucre, as well as the salvation of the souls of his fellow-men.

On Main street, in the vicinity of the hotel, nearly all the principal business houses are situated. That of Mr. Jennings, to which I have already alluded, is but one of a number of large stores. Walker Brothers, Ramshoff & Co., Gllbert & Sons, are the principal Gentile merchants, but the last named *Gentile* firm are also *Jews*. There is known no distinction between Jew and Christian by the Mormon—they are both Gentiles to him. There are a number

---

* Since this was written another hotel, known as the Revere House, has been started by a Gentile, and I understand at least one other will be opened next summer. Gentile houses, I should think, would do well, as the majority of the patrons of the Salt Lake House are anti-Mormons.

of other firms who have no sympathy with Mormonism, that conduct a large and profitable business. The firm I first mentioned have apostatized from the faith and left the church. The immediate cause of the rupture was Brigham Young's dissatisfaction with the amount of tithing they paid, he claiming that it was not one-tenth of their entire profits. This is one striking instance of a growing dissatisfaction arising from this church extortion. The amount of business done in Salt Lake City will probably astonish most of my readers. In 1865 the purchases of Jennings amounted to $460,000; while there are half-a-dozen firms at least, that exceeded $200,000 in their purchases, and this is the cost of the goods in the East, to which must be added the immense cost of transportation from the Atlantic almost across the continent.

There are also several photographic establishments in the city, all owned by Mormons. Savage & Ottinger have the best, and are really good artists. They probably realize a much larger income from the sale of views, and cards of the distinguished men in the church, than from the work they do for individuals. They charge five dollars a dozen for the cards they keep for sale, and the same if an individual has a sitting. Large as is the business done by these merchants, many will be surprised to learn that their stores are conducted upon the plan of country and village stores in the States. Every variety of goods, wares and implements are sold in each establishment, and to Jennings' is added the business of the broker also. In the same store, a customer may purchase anything, from a threshing-machine to a box of Ayers' pills; from a costly silk dress, or pair of white satin slippers, to a sack of potatoes or a pound of brown soap; and the articles purchased may be paid for in coin, gold dust, greenbacks, Mormon shinplasters, flour, grain, pumpkins, cabbages, etc. Such articles of produce form the circulating medium everywhere. A saint from the country will bring in a load of pumpkins, and cabbage, and first he will turn in the tenth of them to the tithing office; then he will make his purchases at the stores, and pay for them in the same, and then he will to go the theatre, with a wife hold of one arm, and a pumpkin under the other to pay for his ticket

Prices are very high. An ordinary cooking-stove sells for one hundred and fifty to one hundred and seventy-five dollars; common cane-seat chairs, seventy-five dollars for a set of six; plain pine bedsteads for sixty dollars; ingrain carpet for three and a half dollars per yard. Groceries and produce command the following prices: Good ham, one dollar per pound; bacon, seventy-five cents; coffee, eighty cents; tea, from three to five dollars; dried fruit, fifty to seventy-five cents; syrup, six to eight dollars per gallon, &c. But the productions of the territory range at lower figures. Beef, fifteen to twenty cents per pound; mutton, a few cents higher; butter, fifty cents; new potatoes, one and a half dollars per bushel; onions, carrots, radishes, &c., cheap.

Three newspapers are published in the city. The "*Vedette*" is an anti-Mormon sheet, which a few months ago was conducted with very little regard for decency or propriety. Under its present management it does better. This paper was started by General Connor, and for a long time indulged in the most unwarranted abuse of the Mormons. The "*Telegraph*" is a Mormon paper, and the "*Deseret News*" the official organ of the church. The two former have daily issue, and the latter appears only weekly.

CHAPTER XIII.

THE DEAD SEA OF AMERICA.

On the second day after my arrival at Camp Douglas, Captain Grimes, the obliging and efficient quartermaster, furnished a handsome "turn out" of four fine horses and a Santa Fé ambulance, and, with one companion, I was soon dashing over Jordan, in the direction of the Great Salt Lake.

But before we go to the Lake, as I may not have occasion again to refer to Camp Douglas or its officers, I will take the present opportunity of alluding to some of them. Colonel Lewis is *the* officer, par excellence, of his battalion. I met him for the first time at Fort Kearney, as I stated in a previous letter, and the favorable impressions then formed have only been increased, after three months' association with him in a subordinate capacity. If it were not for the fear of displeasing him, or bringing a blush to his modest face, I would venture to mention wherein I consider him *one of the best officers*, of any rank, with whom I have served. Opportunities often make men, and it is only for the want of an opportunity that his name is not now familiar to the country as a prominent officer during the war. During all that time he was serving on the frontier. I should not do justice to my feelings if I said less of him, and even this allusion may meet his disapprobation.

Major Benham was another to whom I became attached on the march. For bravery, honesty and unselfishness he cannot be excelled. He is a little reserved to a stranger, but a true friend when he forms an attachment, and as a company officer, among the best in his regiment.

Captain McClintock was, perhaps, my most intimate associate, and a very companionable gentleman, as well as a good officer. His charming lady, who accompanied us through, was esteemed by every one, and every one who esteemed her loved the lovely little Ettie, a sweet infant daughter, who made the journey in the first half-year of her existence.

But I must drop personalities and go on with my visit to the Lake. It is about eighteen miles from the city to Black Rock, a noted landmark on the beach, near where the California road first strikes the border of the lake. The lake is about eighty or ninety miles in length, from north to south, and about sixty in its greatest width from east to west. It contains a number of islands, that rise from the water to mountain heights. The most southern of them is known as Church Island, where the herds belonging to the church, or to the Prophet, are sent to graze. Like the Dead Sea of Palestine, its water is intensely salt, and no living thing is found in it. The quantity of chloride of sodium (common salt) held in solution, is greater than in any body of water in the world. The density of the water of the Dead Sea is a little greater than that of Salt Lake. A comparative analysis of the solid constitutents of the two is as follows:

DEAD SEA.		SALT LAKE.	
Chloride of sodium,	10,390	Chloride of sodium,	20,196
Do. calcium,	3,920	Sulphate of soda,	1,834
Do. magnesium,	10,246	Do. magnesium,	,252
Sulphate of soda,	,054		
			22,282
	24,580		

Thus it appears that, while the Dead Sea has of solid contents a fraction over two per cent. above that of Great Salt Lake, the proportion of common salt in the latter is nearly double that of the former.

Like the Dead Sea, Salt Lake has no outlet, and is constantly supplied with fresh water by several streams. The Jordan, running from Utah Lake, in the early summer months pours into it a body of water almost equal to that carried by its Asiatic namesake from the Sea of Galilee to the Dead Sea of Palestine. The Weber and Bear rivers, to which I have before referred, also empty their waters into Salt Lake. This large supply is not more than sufficient to counterbalance the loss by evaporation, except during the spring and early summer months, when the lake sometimes overflows its borders; nor does the large quantity of fresh water constantly pouring into it lessen its saltness, but, on the contrary, adds to its density. This is explained as follows: all the water of the several streams that empty into the lake have more or less of the solid contents enumerated in the above analysis, and as only a trace of any of these passes off by evaporation, the percentage of common salt remaining in the lake becomes greater rather than less, and nearly reaches the quantity contained in a saturated solution.

Salt works have been established along the lake, and the finest salt I ever saw is obtained simply by driving off the water by boiling. The yield is enormously large, but cannot be as much as is claimed by those engaged in collecting it. They represent that three barrels of water will leave one barrel of salt; but as I have shown there is only twenty-two per cent. of all the solid contents combined, it would not produce more than one-fifth its weight or bulk. The water is of a greenish-blue color, and very transparent, and along the shore there is a peculiar odor, caused by the moisture in the air from the evaporating waters, as well as the decay of myriads of little insects. Near the Black Rock is the usual bathing-place, where the beach is sandy and the bottom free from rocks or irregularities. The lake here is very shallow, and it required me to wade a long distance before I was floated off my feet in the erect posture. Being tired of wading so far, I undertook to swim, but I soon discovered that I was kicking above the surface, with my head very much inclined to assume a lower position, and as the air did not offer resistance sufficient for such locomotion, I had to abandon swimming. I waded on as before, until I accomplished my object—that is, until I could wade no further, not because the water covered me, but because I couldn't reach the bottom with my feet—and there I was, bobbing about on the waves, head and neck above them, like an empty bottle. Turning upon my back, I found less difficulty in swimming, and when in that position, I remembered the description of a bath in the Dead Sea by the editor of the *Advocate*, and remaining perfectly passive, holding my hands up before me, realized that I could have reclined there and read the morning paper with comparative ease. I found a disposition to roll over, face downward, but except this no inconvenience resulted. To sink was impossible, that is, if I lay passive on the water. Wherever there was an abrasion of the skin a smarting sensation was produced. I have been amused at the experience of an English traveller, who, for experiment, opened his eyes beneath the water, and suffered very considerable inconvenience from the smarting and flow of tears that followed. I will not further describe my bath. Let the reader read Dr. Newman's book, "From Dan to Beersheba" and he will be much better pleased with his account of a bath in the Dead Sea than with anything I might write, though my experience was very similar. Before going into the lake, I took the precaution to have some fresh water brought from a neighboring spring, with which to wash the salty solution from my body, and soon saw the utility of the precaution. Neglecting to include my hair in the washing, I found it filled with a fine white powder of salt. The bath altogether was one of the most pleasant I ever had. The temperature of the water was delightful, and after remaining immersed for half an hour, I left it feeling invigorated and refreshed rather than debilitated.

There seems to be a difference of opinion about the buoyancy of the water of this remarkable lake. Captain Burton is the only individual I have ever seen, or read of, or heard of, who did not float on its surface, when bathing in it, and his statement seems a little equivocal. He says he found no *difficulty* in sinking; neither would we find any difficulty in sinking a stick of soft wood for a moment in the Mississippi or North River if one should be dropped from a pier or a boat perpendicularly to the water. I have no idea that the body of a man, if he jumped on the water, would rebound like a rubber ball when struck against a marble slab; but I am very much inclined to think that if the gentleman named has five pounds of fat in his whole corpus some part of it would float above water.

But the tendency of writers is to exaggerate the other way; they represent the water to be more buoyant than it is. Certainly it is remarkable enough without exaggerating to furnish subject-matter for an interesting letter; then why spoil the whole by overreaching possibilities. One writer says: "With my hands clasped together under my head, and my feet crossed, I floated upon the very surface of the lake with at least one-third of my body above water." My experience was quite different. I could not have remained in such a position for a moment, but would have rolled over, face downward, and if my hands were retained behind my head it would have put my face under water. If the weight of my body had been such as to make it more buoyant, then there would have been still greater difficulty. I doubt further whether cold water, under any circumstances, can hold in solution mineral constituents sufficient to increase its density until it would float a living, healthy human body one-third above the surface.

Nor do I believe that a person cannot drown in Salt Lake. Knowing how to swim I found no difficulty in keeping my head above the water, but I think if I had not been so experienced in deep water I would have found considerable difficulty in doing so. I believe if a person should fall from a boat, and lose the erect posture, his head, being the heavier part, wouldgo under, and the man drown, as his body floated on the surface. This is merely a matter of opinion, however, and it might be demonstrated to be erroneous.

Feeling highly gratified with the morning's experience we started back for the city, stopping at a neat-looking little house near by, from which was displayed a sign, reading "Meals furnished at Seasonable Hours;" but we took only a glass of buttermilk, and regarded it as an unseasonable hour for our dinner, though the family were then partaking. The house was kept by a Mormon lady whose daughter's appearance rather attracted my companion. As we hurried across the plain to escape rather an unusual thing at that season—a rain-storm—with that magnificent team dashing along at the rate of ten miles an hour, I thought that Major Grimes, who furnished it, ought to be Quartermaster-General.

Another curiosity in the vicinity of Salt Lake City is the hot spring. It is a few miles north of the warm springs I alluded to in my last, and situated at the base of the same range of hills or spur of the mountains. It pours out quite a large stream of water from an opening in the solid rock, but a few feet distant from the road. Running through a drain which has been dug to prevent the road from being flooded, it spreads out into a pretty lake which is a favorite resort for large numbers of wild ducks in the fall, and in the winter it is the grand natural skating park of Salt Lake City. Where the water escapes from the rock the temperature of it is at least 130 degrees, and several feet distant it was so uncomfortably hot as not to permit me holding my hand in it for a second. I resorted to the popular test of hot water in such springs, and put in some eggs to boil, but as the process of coagulating was going on rather slowly, and night approaching more rapidly, with several bad places in the road to the city, and a demoralized driver, because he was kept out so late, I abandoned the experiment and left my eggs for the breakfast of the first emigrant who should pass in the morning, if he felt inclined to indulge in the luxury. But I fancy, if he were a Gentile, he supposed they had been poisoned, and put there by a Mormon, and if a Mormon, that the same diabolical act had been done by a Gentile, and the eggs were probably not disturbed.

A tale is told of a miner from Montana, whose love for the saints in Utah was not of a very high order (as is the case with miners generally), who passed the spring on his way to the city. Before doing so, however, he concluded to take a bath without trying the temperature of the water in the spring itself, though he had done so in the drain a few yards from it. A Mormon happened to be passing along at the time, and seeing that the man was laboring under some mistake, or crazy, went to him, kindly remarking that *he couldn't bathe there.* This aroused the Gentile, who very indignantly responded, with sundry oaths, that he would do anything in that country that a Mormon could do. He thought the man questioned his right to use the spring, and continuing his disrobing, stepped into the water up to his knees, to jump out again with a good deal more agility than when he stepped in, very much to the amusement of the saint, and to the gratification of his feelings of revenge for the cursing he got. The miner had been informed by some friends of the warm springs, and the luxury of a bath in them, and as that was before the days of bathing-houses in that vicinity, he had simply mistaken the locality.

The smell of sulphureted hydrogen could be detected for some distance from the spring, and its action upon a silver coin turned it black in a few minutes. The smell is said to be particularly objectionable to some animals, and I am told that it is often difficult to drive a horse through the little stream that crosses the road.

This is a country of lakes, and not least among the many to be admired for natural beauty, and that of its surroundings, is a lake in the top of the mountains. A short distance south of the "Twin Peaks," almost on the very summit of the Wasach Mountains, is found Cotton-Wood Lake. It is reached by a wagon road on the western slope, which enters a cañon a few miles south of Parley, and on the east can be approached by a trail leading over the mountains from Parley's Park. The scenery along the western approach is very wild and sublime. On one side of the road are almost perpendicular walls of solid rock hundreds of feet high, and on the other side the rushing, leaping waters of the outlet of the lake, which are lashed into a foam as they run over the rocks, giving it the appearance of a stream of snow, or a glacier after it has dashed against rocks to grind it as fine and white. Making a steep ascent along a narrow road, until you reach an altitude of four thousand feet above the valley, you come upon this beautiful little lake. The banks on the east are tall and steep, but on the western side, for a short distance, the land is almost level with the surface of the lake. The water is as clear as crystal, and the trout can be seen swimming through it as distinctly as the gold-fish in the pools of parks in eastern cities, while the bottom is very plainly seen where it is ten or twelve feet deep. Trout-fishing here is not so exciting as in the rapid streams. The water is still, and the fish seem to partake of the sluggishness of their element. The hooks must be sunk, as the trout will not come to the surface, and then when he bites he does so as deliberately as if it were a dainty morsel, and you can see him as he takes the bait in his mouth and runs off. How different from the way he bites in the rapid streams! There, as soon as the bait touches the surface, and indeed sometimes before, he will jump entirely out of the water and catch it, perfectly electrifying the sportsman.

I did not fish in Cotton-Wood Lake; but a few days before my arrival at Camp Douglas, several officers made an excursion there, and brought away the finny tribe by the hundreds. It was then the month of July, the reader will remember, and they obtained snow from a bank within a few hundred yards of the lake in which they packed the fish to preserve them as they returned through the warm valley. If the reader ever visits Cotton-Wood Lake in the summer, to encamp for the night, I would advise him by all means to go furnished with a mosquito-bar, for I think there is more danger of being carried off bodily by the little insects there, than in any place I have visited.

While referring to the natural phenomena of this locality, I must mention the gorgeous sunsets that may be observed from Camp Douglas. Salt Lake, it will be remembered, is west of the post, and during the earlier hours of the day is but indistinctly seen, and its surface is distinguished from the land around by its dark appearance; but on a clear afternoon, as the sun is about disappearing behind it, or, apparently, in the lake, the water is lit up with a brilliancy that makes it look like a sea of mercury. As if rising out of the lake, the sky by the same reflection assumes a similar appearance, and the borders of the fleecy clouds which hang about the horizon become as brilliant as polished gold, and constantly changing in shape as well as in the different hues of their bright colors. The sight fills the observer with wonder and amazement, as he admires their beauty. The same reflection also lights up the outlines of the mountain islands, and after gazing intently upon the scene, I could not define the termination of the water from the beginning of the sky, nor distinguish between the shining mountains and the shining clouds. Italian skies and seas could not have presented a more gorgeous sunset.

This letter concludes my description of the journey and what I saw; in those to follow I will endeavor to tell the reader what I have learned about one of the most remarkable people of modern times.

CHAPTER XIV.

THE MORMON CHURCH.

A HISTORY of the Mormon Church, condense it as I might, so as to give a tolerably clear idea of what it has been, what it has done, and what it teaches at the present day, would of itself make a book. What I shall write, therefore, may be regarded as merely fragmentary; but it is a subject of too much interest, for one writing from Utah, to pass over without some notice.

I shall endeavor to present to the reader such facts connected with the history of this strange people, and such incidents of both their inner and outward life, as have passed under my observation, or come to my knowledge through reliable channels.

I will discard the extravagant and unsubstantiated stories which are constantly in the mouths of anti-Mormons, who, from prejudice arising from a real or imaginary injury, can see nothing in the lives or characters of individuals holding allegiance to Brigham Young, but to despise and contemn, and are constantly traducing them. I started for Utah with a very superficial knowledge of the Mormons, and with my mind made up not to prejudge them upon the mere hearsay evidence of their enemies, but determined to see and learn of them for myself, and not to base my opinion upon the mere opinion of others. The result was that my first impressions of them were favorable. They appeared exceedingly plausible, and in nine cases out of ten the liberal Gentile is impressed as I was, and will endeavor to cover up, and explain away, very much that he learns from the more experienced that is prejudicial to the characters of the leaders of the sect. Such at least was my experience, and I have had many long and sharp arguments in defence of what I supposed was an injured and abused people.

Much of their true history I was reluctant to believe, but fact after fact has been presented so clearly before me, that I am compelled to change the opinions first formed. Nor am I alone in this respect either; but I find nearly every intelligent and honest individual who has taken the trouble to look into their iniquitous system, and at first thought of them as I did, has been led to think of them as I do now.

I am sorry to believe that much that has been written abusive of the Mormons, has been so colored by prejudice, as I have before intimated, as to distort facts, and by extravagant descriptions destroy the effect which a plain statement would have upon the thoughtful reader.

Then on the other hand the extreme plausibility of the leaders, with their apparent liberality, and their hospitable treatment of influential strangers, cause others to state as much *less* than the truth, as the first class state more. They are led to consider them as not near so bad as they are represented to be, and not unnaturally side with the weaker party. They have heard extravagant abuse until they are willing to conceal much that they must abhor as an offset.

Before referring to the church as it exists at the present day, I will give a brief sketch of its history from its origin.

Mormonism had its rise in New Hampshire in 1830, when Joseph Smith claims to have received and translated the Book of Mormon, and organized the Church of Latter Day Saints. Smith declared himself to have been specially inspired for the work, and designated by the Almighty as the leader of His people. He claims to have received the revelation from God, written in mystic characters upon plates of gold, and his translation of the inscriptions thereon is the Mormon Bible of the present day. Missionaries were at once sent out to proclaim the new gospel. As evidence of their divine authority they pretended to work miracles. Early in its history the new sect was subjected to rigid persecution, which only increased their fanaticism, and Joseph Smith soon entertained the idea of establishing a temporal sovereignty. The character of Smith had been notoriously bad for years before he claimed to be the great revelator of a new gospel. His reputation for veracity suffered alike with his reputation for violating the laws of the country prohibiting larceny, while almost the entire community in which he resided regarded him as devoid of principle and honesty. He was a visionary gold-seeker, digging everywhere for the metal, and coveting wealth with the least possible amount of labor that might be expended in gaining it. The various doctrines to which the church now hold were submitted and adopted from time to time, and early in its history an important work styled "Book of Doctrines and Covenants" was written, which is claimed to consist of revelations received since the publication of the Book of Mormon, and is accepted still as a rule of faith and practice, with such modifications as it is claimed subsequent revelations have made to its teaching.

These pretended revelations, as will be seen hereafter, have made very radical changes in the practices of the church, and their religious tenets seem to be as susceptible of as different interpretations as a treaty, or the constitution of the United States in these times.

The Church soon attempted to establish a local independent government of its own (as it has *de facto* in Utah at present), but soon found itself in conflict with the lawful authority of the land. The practices of the Mormons were not only unlawful, but often so disgusting to the people of Illinois and Missouri as to bring about violence. Unfortunately the passions of a mob so ruled as to result in the murder of Smith, the leader, in Nauvoo, Illinois, in

1844. At the time of his death, he was in prison for violation of law, when the prison was forced, and the man shot dead on the spot. John Taylor, now one of the Apostles in Salt Lake City, narrowly escaped being killed at the same time. He was a fellow-prisoner of Smith's, and a ball passed through his clothing and lodged in his watch, which he still preserves as a memento of the tragedy. Such acts are always to be deprecated. Mob violence is barbarism, whether in the acts of a Vigilance Committee in California, a massacre in New Orleans, or the attempt of a John Brown to incite insurrection in a peaceable community.

Brigham Young, now the Prophet, President, Seer and Revelator was received into the church in the second year of its existence, and in 1835 was elected President of the "Twelve Apostles."

After the death of Joseph Smith, Sidney Rigdon, one of his councillors, assumed the Presidency; but before he had ruled a year he was deposed by Brigham. It appears that no "revelation" had been recorded, providing for a successor in the event of the death of the Prophet, and Rigdon being next highest in rank, naturally claimed the position. As there was then no one individual to receive a revelation that would satisfy the clashing interest of aspirants, Brigham Young proposed to show the will of God concerning the succession by a miraculous demonstration. So on one occasion Brigham went into the pulpit, to preach, as he had often done before, and upon rising before the congregation, he assumed the appearance, manners and tone of voice of Joseph Smith, the martyr, so perfectly as to quite electrify the people. Whereupon it was at once conceded that the mantle had fallen upon him, and he was by acclamation declared to be the President of the Church. This made poor Rigdon to be an impostor, and he was cut off and delivered over to the buffetings of Satan. Brigham Young's course met the disapprobation of Emma Smith, who had been the *public* wife of Joseph. She contended then, as she does now, that her husband had expressly declared, that at his death his mantle would fall upon his oldest son, and he become the leader in Israel. The people loved Joseph, and revered his memory, and had it not been for the powers of mimicry of Young, the counsel of Emma would probably have prevailed, and long ere this he would have been a subject of Joseph II., or more probably the Church would long since have ceased to exist. The miraculous demonstration, as the prophet regarded it, was beyond any assurances Emma could give them of what had been the wishes of the Prophet, and they accepted it as indisputable evidence that a greater than Joseph willed it otherwise.

Finding their existence as a sect in jeopardy if they remained in Illinois and Missouri, they soon after the death of Smith, sought a more congenial country. In April 1847, the pioneer band of saints, numbering 143 men, headed by the President, left the Missouri River for a new Zion in the Far West. In the fall of that year they reached Salt Lake Valley, and Brigham, from a peak of the Wasach Mountains, saw the country, and had a vision in which he was told that this was to be their future Zion, where the Temple of the Lord was again to be erected never to be removed, and that the light of the Gospel was to radiate thence to all the world. That fall the city was laid out, and they immediately commenced preparing for the reception of the hosts of Zion who were to follow.

Brigham Young returned to the Missouri River, and in 1848 he was confirmed by a General Conference of the Church in the position to which he had been called by the people on the occasion referred to. In the same year Young returned to Salt Lake City, taking with him the great mass of the Mormons. These people had then collected on the banks of the Missouri, opposite Council Bluffs, preparatory to their migration to the land which Brigham told them was to flow with milk and honey, equalled only by the Promised Land, which Moses was allowed to look upon but not possess. That they did not find it to be all their imaginations pictured, I have already stated. They endured great hardships on the journey, and intense suffering after their arrival. They were short of provisions, and before they could cultivate the land, they lived on beetles, and grasshoppers, and such nutritious wild herbs as could be found. They were very poorly clad, and without shelter, and a long and dreary winter, colder than they ever before experienced, was upon them. Was it surprising that they murmured? But out of all their difficulties Brigham Young managed to deliver them. As soon as it could be done the people commenced agricultural pursuits. But when the husbandmen could not work, they were employed in other ways, and snch as could not labor advantageously on any *necessary* work, were made to labor on the "Bulwarks of Zion."

Nothing better proves the ability of Brigham Young as the leader of a fanatical religious sect, and as a man of most extraordinary resources, than the management of the migration of the Mormons, and of their affairs during the first year of their arrival in the valley.

At that time Utah was a part of Mexico. By a treaty between that Government and the United States, the territory was ceded to the latter, and in 1849 the Mormons met in convention, adopted a constitution which they called "The Constitution of the State of Deseret," and applied for immediate admission into the Union under it. There was then no recognized government in that country; but the year following Congress organized the present territory, and Mr. Fillmore, who was then President, appointed Brigham Young the first Governor as well as Commissioner of Indian Affairs.

It has ever been a fundamental idea with the Mormon leaders, that the church and state should really be one government, however distinct they might nominally be made, and it has been so to this date.

One would suppose, under their territorial organization, with their President as Governor, and a legislature entirely of the church, the Mormons would no longer continue their quasi State government. But nevertheless it has continued, and on the twenty-second of January last "The General Assembly of the State of Deseret" memoralized Congress for the admission of Utah into the Union, with the constitution adopted in 1849 slightly amended.* They evidently foresaw the danger of Brigham's removal from office. As a State he could always be the Governor.

Utah being in the very centre of the Indian country of the West, for several years after its settlement by the Mormons the colonies were subjected to Indian outrages. Wherever a settlement was made the first work of the settlers was to build a fort.

But from the organization of the territory in 1850, nothing remarkable in the history of the saints occurred until 1857, when their usurpation of authority, and defiance of law, as well as their hostility to officers who were not of their faith (particularly the Judiciary), led to the withdrawal of all

* The following is an extract from a letter written by one of the most prominent apostles to explain why the memorial was presented. The letter appears in the *Telegraph* of February 28, 1867:

"In my late travels through this district, I have often been asked the question: 'Why did the Legislative Assembly again memoralize Congress for the admission of the territory into the Union as a State, after having so often done so before and so often been rejected?' My answer has been, 'We wish to do the will of Heaven by asking for those rights and privileges which the Most High hath vouchsafed to us in the constitution of our common country. When forced away from our homes in Missouri, we were commanded of the Lord to importune for redress at the feet of the Judge, and if he heeded us not, we were required to importune at the feet of the Governor; and if the Governor heeded us not, then we were to importune at the feet of the President; and if he heeded us not, then would the Lord arise and come out of his hiding-place, and in his fury vex the nation, and in his hot displeasure, and in his fierce anger, in his time, would cut off those wicked, unfaithful, and unjust stewards, and appoint them their portion among hypocrites and unbelievers; even in outer darkness, where there is weeping and wailing and gnashing of teeth.'

"The foregoing instructions were given to the church in the month of December, 1833 (see Book of Covenants, third European edition, page 283, section 12). Since the date of the commandment referred to, has the nation been vexed with a sore vexation, and is it still vexed? Have many rulers singularly disappeared from their official stations? These questions inspire grief and sorrow in every feeling breast; so much so that I answer them not, but leave the reader to furnish his own answer."

So our national troubles are made by this writer to be attributable to the failure of the Government in the discharge of its duty to the Latter Day Saints, and it is intimated that President Lincoln and others have been sent to hell for denying to them their rights. The writer further remarks that the continued refusal of Congress "will cause the nation to mourn more sadly than it ever yet has done."

such officers from the territory. The overt act, that brought about the bloodless "Mormon War," was the seizure of the records of the United States courts in the office of Judge Styles, one of the associate Justices of the territory. This was done by order of the President, during the absence of the Judge from his office, and the parties who carried out the President's instructions also destroyed the private property of the Judge. Soon thereafter Judge Styles withdrew from the territory and reported the fact at Washington. Mr. Buchanan then appointed other territorial officers in the place of Mormons, including Governor A. Cumming to relieve Brigham Young. The Secretary of War was directed to send a sufficient body of troops with the Governor to the territory to act as a *posse comitatus* in requiring the enforcement of the laws.

Nothing more was contemplated. It was not the intention of the Government to inflict upon the Mormons any punishment for their past lawlessness, but to make them more mindful of law in the future, by stationing this body of troops in the territory. The commanding officer of the expedition expected no opposition to the march of his forces into the territory, and was so fully of the impression that they would submit quietly, that he sent an officer in advance of the column to purchase grain in Salt Lake City for the army upon its arrival there.

Brigham Young, however, regarded it as a hostile movement, and not only refused to sell the officer supplies, but upon the day of his arrival in the city issued his proclamation declaring martial law, and calling out the militia to resist a "hostile force who are evidently assailing us (the Mormons) to accomplish our destruction and overthrow."

The army marched onward, until it arrived in the vicinity of where Fort Bridger now stands, when their supplies became scant because of trains failing to come up, and the capture of some by the Mormons, and they encamped on Black's Fork for the winter. While there Brigham addressed a communication to the then Colonel A. Sidney Johnston (who afterward distinguished himself and lost his life in the rebel army), warning him to leave the territory by the same route he entered; but in the event Colonel Johnston desired to remain over winter, he might "do so in peace and unmolested," provided he would deposit his arms and ammunition with the Quartermaster-General of the territory, and "leave in the spring, or as soon as the roads would permit him to march." It is unnecessary to add, that neither modest request was complied with. While the army was approaching, the Mormons were fortifying Echo Canon, to prevent its penetrating further into the territory.

The only act of hostility committed during the campaign, was the destruction of two supply trains, belonging to Johnston's army. This was done by a band of horsemen, supposed to have been commanded by Porter Rockwell, who figures conspicuously in Mormon history as one of the Danites, or "avenging angels."

General Johnston was not acting under orders to attack the Mormons, even if he had been so situated as to do so advantageously, and this act of hostility would have been a most excellent pretext for accepting war, and then and forever settling the question of Mormonism in our country, if it had been at a season when it could have been taken advantage of. Neither the defences of Echo Cañon, nor the size of the Mormon army, were by any means the cause of it not being. The army was short of supplies, as I have already stated, and the severity of the winter prevented all aggressive measures. Before the time arrived when the army could have acted, a semi-Mormon succeeded in arranging for an interview between Brigham Young and Governor Cumming, in Salt Lake City, when the exceeding plausibility of the former so favorably impressed the Governor, that he immediately communicated the result of his interview to the President, when a commission was sent out to treat with Brigham. He satisfied them of his loyalty, and produced the records of the courts, which he had only stolen and not destroyed. The diplomacy of Brigham was equal to the occasion, and very speedily an agreement was entered into by which the command of General Johnston was allowed to march through Salt Lake City and establish Camp Floyd, about forty miles distant.

This large body of troops in the territory scattered hundreds of thousands of dollars throughout the country, and when the army was withdrawn a large quantity of supplies, with mules and wagons, were disposed of for mere nominal sums. In some places bacon was sold at one dollar for sacks containing a hundred pounds, when the retail price of the article was seventy-five cents per pound.

The Mormon expedition, then, resulted in incalculable pecuniary benefit to the people, in still further demonstation of the ability of their leader, and in strengthening their confidence in their cause and their ability to resist the Government, which may yet lead to bloodshed and their ruin.

I should have stated that Brigham Young yielded gracefully the *nominal* Governorship of the territory to Governor Cumming at the first interview they had.

Since the troops entered Utah in 1857, the Mormons have been under but little better subjugation. They have not been quite so open and bold in their opposition to the Government as before, but notwithstanding there is a secret hatred and defiance of it, so deeply rooted in them, that it cannot be removed as long as their present system exists. A remedy for the evil I will discuss in a future letter.

CHAPTER XV.

DOCTRINE OF THE MORMON CHURCH.—POLYGAMY.

HAVING reviewed in the last letter the political history of the Mormons, I now submit something concerning their teachings and practices of the present day.

Their published articles of faith are as follows:

1. "We believe in God, the Eternal Father; and his Son Jesus Christ, and in the Holy Ghost.

2. "We believe that men will be punished for their own sins, and not for Adam's transgressions.

3. "We believe that through the Atonement of Christ all mankind may be saved by obedience to the laws and ordinances of the Gospel.

4. "We believe these ordinances are, 1st, Faith in the Lord Jesus; 2nd, Repentance; 3d, Baptism by immersion for the remission of sins; 4th, Laying on of hands by the gift of the Holy Spirit; 5th, the "Lord's Supper."

5. "We believe that man must be called of God by inspiration, and by laying on of hands from those who are duly commissioned to preach the Gospel and administer in the Ordinances thereof.

6. "We believe in the same organization that existed in the primitive Church, viz: Apostles, Prophets, Pastors, Evangelists, etc.

7. "We believe in the powers and gifts of the everlasting Gospel, viz: the Gift of Faith, discerning of Spirits, prophecy, revelations, visions, healing, tongues, and the interpretation of tongues, wisdom, charity, brotherly love, etc.

8. "We believe the word of God recorded in the Bible; we also believe the Word of God recorded in the Book of Mormon, and in all other good books.

9. "We believe all that God has revealed, all that he does now reveal, and we believe that he will reveal many more great and important things pertaining to the Kingdom of God and Messiah's second coming.

10. "We believe in the literal gathering of Israel and in the restoration of the Ten Tribes; that Zion will be established upon the Western Continent, and that Christ will reign personally upon the earth for a thousand years; and that the earth will be renewed and receive its paradisiacal glory.

11. "We believe in the literal resurrection of the body, and that the rest of the dead live not again until the thousand years are expired.

12. "We claim the privilege of worshipping Almighty God according to the dictates of conscience unmolested, and

allow all men the same privilege, let them worship how or when they may.

13. "We believe in being subject to Kings, Queens, Presidents, Rulers, and Magistrates, in obeying, honoring and sustaining the law.

14. "We believe in being honest, true, chaste, temperate, benevolent, virtuous, and upright, and in doing good to all men; indeed, we may say that we follow the admonition of Paul; we believe all things, we hope all things, we have endured very many things and hope to be able to endure all things. Everything lovely, virtuous, praiseworthy, and of good report, we seek after, looking forward to the recompense of reward; but an idle or lazy person cannot be a Christian, neither have salvation. He is a drone, and destined to be stung to death, and tumbled out of the hive."

This strange admixture of doctrines, culled from the tenets of almost every religious, as well as pagan sect, is modified from time to time to better suit their materialistic views, increase the despotism of the church, and sanction their lustful pleasures.

There are many very absurd doctrines now taught, which are not warranted by the articles I have quoted nor taught in their original works on theology. Materialism is hinted at in the articles; but is very plainly taught in some of their writings as well as in their discourses. Orson Pratt, one of the "Twelve," a noted writer in the church, and expounder of the faith, and perhaps the smartest man among them, in explaining their belief in this particular, is guilty of the following irreverent and profane language, as recorded in "*The Seer*," a work edited by him and published in Liverpool:

"The Father is a material being. The substance of His person occupies space. It has mobility, length, breadth and thickness, like other matter. The substance of His person cannot be in two places at the same time. It requires time for him to transport himself from place to place." Again he says: "The resemblance between God and man has reference to shape and figure. Man has legs and so has God, as it is evident from His appearance to Abraham. Man walks with his legs, so does God. God cannot only walk but He can move up and down through the air without using his legs. He can waft himself from world to world by His self-moving power," etc.

On this same subject I might quote higher authority than Orson Pratt. During the visit of Mr. Colfax to Salt Lake City in 1865, he requested the President to preach a sermon on the doctrines of the church, and Mr. Colfax went the next day to the tabernacle to hear him. In this sermon, Mr. Bowles reports him as having said:

"That God was a human natural person, with like flesh and blood and passions as ourselves, only perfect in all things; that He begot his Son Jesus in the same way children are begotten now; that Jesus and the Father looked alike, only the Father looked older."

Concerning the materiality of the third person in the Trinity, the writer I first cited remarks:

"The Holy Ghost is also a material substance. It exists in vast immeasurable quantities in all natural worlds. God the Father, and God the Son cannot be everywhere present; indeed they cannot be in two places at the same time; but God the Holy Spirit is omnipresent. No one atom of the Holy Spirit can be in two places at the same instant. Each atom is intelligent, and like other matter has validity, etc. If several atoms of the Spirit should exist united together in the form of a person, then this person of the Holy Spirit would be subject to the same necessity as the other two persons in the Godhead; that is, it could not be everywhere present," etc.

They also teach that Adam is the God of this world, and I believe they make it out in some way that he was a polygamist.

Referring to Adam, reminds me of an individual, a little more crazy than most Mormons, who imagined himself to be God of this world. He had had a wife who was not much sounder in mind. It seemed to be a monomania with him as he was a man of some education and of certainly ordinary intelligence on most subjects, but he contended that Adams' spirit had transmigrated into his body, and that he had been six thousand years looking for Eve, whom he found only the year before I saw him. Eve, it seems, had been acting badly according to his own statement, for when he found her, he said she had become a base prostitute; but he intended to elevate her to her proper position in society. He declared her to be his mate; so decreed from the beginning of time, but he treated her in the most barbarous manner, explaining that it was all intended to give her a proper idea of her inferiority. For this reason, or some other, Adam cut her hair short to her head, and pulled out all her teeth. They started together, on foot, for the States from Salt Lake City, and as such garments were more convenient for pedestrians, he dressed her in men's clothes. There is no asylum in Utah for providing for this class of citizens, and if there were, I doubt whether they could have the benefit of it, as they were not orthodox Mormons, but Josephites. But this is digressing from the subject of this letter. To keep the run of the doctrines of the Mormon Church would require a close attention to the teachings of the "Zion of the Lord," and to current revelation; I do not propose to criticize them here as absurd, as many of them are. They are only questions of opinion, and with their opinions I have no disposition to meddle. It is about their practices I have most to say.

After the subject of doctrine, I may as well refer next to their church government. In the Mormon Church there are a greater number and variety of officials than in any other sect with which I am familiar. But, notwithstanding this apparent division of authority, it is probable the greatest ecclesiastical despotism now extant. The head of the church has in his power the lives and property of his deluded followers, and to him all acknowledge the most profound allegiance, while the masses virtually worship him. As he is not nominally the only power in the church, I will proceed to explain the different branches of the hierarchy, which consists of the following:

I. *The Presidency.* This consists of three individuals, Brigham Young, Heber C. Kimball and Daniel H. Wells (the latter also Mayor of Salt Lake City, Secretary of State of the State of Deseret, and Lieutenant-General of the militia of the territory, the act of Congress abolishing such office to the contrary notwithstanding). They are known respectively as the 1st, 2d and 3d presidents, and constitute the supreme power among the Mormons, both in temporal matters and ecclesiastical. Brigham Young is the power that controls the presidency, and the presidency controls the people. They claim divine authority for all their acts, but are elected by the people, the masses of whom regard the first president as unsurpassed in wisdom by any save the Omniscient. His mandate, or, rather, a simple expression of his wishes, without making it a command, is undisputed authority, and is obeyed implicitly. As policy on the part of this autocracy, it is nominally made to be responsible to the twelve apostles; but so implicit is the faith of the apostle, that their judgment and conscience would yield at once if they presumed for a moment to question the wisdom of their seer.

II. *The Patriarch.* This official is one who administers solely in spiritual matters, and his duties consist in bestowing patriarchal blessings upon the faithful who desire them, and are willing to pay for them. He will lay his reverend hands upon the head of a saint, and bless him with houses, and lands, and wives (number specified), and children, and heirship to eternal glory *if faithful.* These blessings are written out and signed by the Patriarch, and are highly prized by the ignorant. Of course, if the holder of the certificate fails to realize all that is promised therein, there is a saving clause for the Patriarch at the conclusion of the blessing, by which the failure is always satisfactorily explained.

John Smith, a nephew of the first prophet, now fills this office, and, making occasional tours through the territory, returns laden with chickens, ducks, homespun cloth, and everything else which is raised or manufactured in the country, which is portable and not immediately perishable. He is supported by such fees.

III. *The Twelve Apostles*, or "special witnesses of the name of Christ in all the world." This body ranks next after the presidency, and have general superintendence of missionary labor. The apostles ordain subordinate officials of the clerical order, baptize, administer the sacrament, and are the principle preachers and expounders of the faith. The names of but few of the "*Twelve*" are familiar to the public, because of any very conspicuous acts, and I will not enumerate them here.

IV. "*The Seventy*" are chosen men for missionary labor, and to build up the church in all her "stakes." There are of the original "seventy" seven presidents elected, who have authority to appoint other seventies, whose presidents may appoint still others, and the number so multiplied *ad infinitum*, or to the extent of the wants of the church for such laborers in the vineyard.

The missionaries are sent out "without purse or scrip," nominally. The amount of it is, their expenses are paid by the people or by themselves, and do not come out of the purse of the church. On this subject I shall say more in a letter on proselyting.

V. *The High Priests.* This is a body of church officials, who are elected to administer principally in spiritual concerns, under the immediate direction of the President. They have authority to officiate in any office when there are none of the properly constituted of such officers present. They are not entirely an ecclesiastical body, as the Bishops and the High Council form part of it. The unbelieving Gentiles say that they do the President's "dirty work," but in what way, if at all, I am unable to say, except upon the authority of general rumor.

VI. *The Bishops.* Their duties pertain more to temporal matters than to ecclesiastical. There is one appointed to every settlement in the territory, and one to every ward in Salt Lake City. They are collectors of tithes, keep the census of their several districts, and settle difficulties existing among the saints, when they can do so, subject to appeal to higher authority. They are supposed to administer to the spiritual wants of the people of their charge, and visit their homes for this purpose. In this respect their duties are made similar to those required of Methodist class-leaders, and are discharged about as inefficiently as the majority of our Methodist brethren discharge theirs. Bishop Hunter is the chief of the Bishops, and is the channel through which any matter of business the Ward Bishop may be unable to settle to the satisfaction of the parties, or any grievance, must be communicated to higher authority.

VII. *The High Council.* This consists of twelve High Priests, with the President of the Church at its head. It is the highest authority to which parties may appeal when they feel aggrieved by the decision of their Bishop or other local authority. The President is required to give the decision in all cases brought before the Council when the others vote upon it. The reader may imagine how far the opinion of one who is thought incapable to err has to do with the vote of the Council. Its jurisdiction is confined to temporal matters.

Litigation, which should properly come before United States courts, which the Mormons decline to recognize further than absolutely compelled to, is decided upon by the High Council, and from this there is no appeal. It is true that such cases might then be taken before a lawful court, but no Mormon dare do such a thing.

Besides the officials of the church here enumerated, there are several other classes, known as Elders, Priests, Teachers, and Deacons; but as the duties of all these are included among those of higher grades, and as they interlace and overlap each other, so I will not occupy more space in referring to them.

It will be seen by the foregoing, that the church is virtually a State organization as much as an ecclesiastical, but it would not be in keeping with the pretended liberality of the church (which I may say is in reality the most illiberal and despotic in the world), to have it appear that the people are governed in their temporal affairs by a church which is governed by one man. So the temporal government is made nominally distinct. Brigham Young being deposed as Governor of the Territory, is still respected as the Governor of the State of Deseret. But no such organization will make the church other than a temporal sovereignty. The President is also the Governor, the High Council is the Supreme Court, and the Bishops the Magistrates or Police Judges.

There are United States territorial officers in Utah, but they are almost impotent to enforce the laws. A case requiring trial by jury would necessitate the impanelling of a jury of Mormons, and under no circumstances would they decide contrary to the teaching of the church, and under no circumstances would a Mormon apply to a United States judge for redress for any grievance, if indeed they could consider any outrage a grievance, after it had been adjudicated by their highest tribunal.

Concerning the ridiculous absurdities of their theology, as well as their church government, I have nothing further to say. Let the reader judge of them from what I have already written. I am not a theologian, and as to religious views, they are as much entitled to their opinions as I am to mine, dissimilar as they are. But allowing them the fullest liberty in this respect, they cannot be permitted to disregard decency and violate law, without being held up to public opprobrium; and if they persist, and other measures fail to remove the *great* evil, then the strong arm of the military power of the Government must be stretched forth; but God forbid that such should ever become necessary.

The one great objectionable feature of Mormonism is polygamy—a system of modern introduction into the church, which is as degrading as it is criminal to all who indulge in it. It is a relic of barbarism, that cannot exist in a civilized and refined community, and to the Mormon Church is the mysterious handwriting upon the wall which tells too plainly the fate of the sect.

Polygamy is not claimed to be a privilege allowed the faithful, but a religious duty enjoined by a divine revelation to Joseph Smith in 1843. Strange as it may seem this duty was not taught to the faithful until nine years after Smith claimed to have received the revelation. It was first promulgated by Brigham Young, and he bungled in getting it before the people. He admits that the original draft of the revelation, as transcribed from the inspired (?) lips of the Prophet, was destroyed by Emma, the wife of Joseph, but fortunately for posterity a certain Bishop, who had been intimate with Smith, had previously borrowed the document, and while in his possession a copy was taken, so the malice of Emma availed her nothing. This copy is Brigham's authority. A profane writer, the editor of the *Salt Lake Telegraph*, refers to polygamy as a doctrine as precious to the Mormons as was "that of a Redeemer born to the Apostles of old;" but notwithstanding its importance it was withheld from the church these nine years, while Brigham claims to have had it in his possession for several. But he says "everything must come in its time, as there is a time for everything," and in the fullness of time" it was made known. When first announced, he admitted that some, who could be trusted with the secret, had been previously let into it, and had enjoyed its privileges. With the announcement of polygamy began the first serious trouble in the church. The Smith family, who had regarded Brigham with jealousy since he first held the position claimed by the son of the first prophet, made this the pretext for organizing a faction, which they claim to be the *true* church of Latter Day Saints. They deny positively and emphatically the reception of a revelation by Smith enjoining polygamy. The controversy so far is rather damaging to both parties. Brigham, and the polygamists generally claiming, not only that Smith was authorized to announce it as a doctrine of the church, but that he practiced it himself. On the other hand the Josephites, or anti-polygamists, point triumphantly to an official publication in the Mormon Journal at Nauvoo, dated February 1, 1844 (the year in which Smith was killed). It reads as follows:—

"NOTICE:

"As we have already been credibly informed that an Elder of the Church of Jesus Christ of Latter Day Saints, by the name of Hiram Brown, has been preaching polygamy, and other false and corrupt doctrines, in the County of Lapier and State of Michigan:

"This is to notify him, and the church in general, that he has been cut off from the church for his iniquity, and he is further notified to appear at the Special Conference on the 6th of April next to answer to these charges.

"JOSEPH SMITH,
"HYRAM SMITH,
"Presidents of the Church."*

Reasoning upon the presumption that Smith was an honest and truthful man (if it is admissible to suppose such a case in the face of the light of history, which makes him a base impostor), Brigham Young must have been deceived, or is himself a deceiver, in attributing to Smith what he had pronounced false and corrupt. Or take the other horn of the dilemma, and believe Brigham Young, then Smith, his great prototype, must have been a base hypocrite and deceiver, and certainly not one who would be ordained of Heaven to establish a kingdom of righteousness upon the earth.

On the same subject, a few months later, in the same year, a bull from Hyram, the second President, seems to have been published for the benefit of a certain community in which this "false and corrupt doctrine" had been taught.

This reads as follows:—

"NAUVOO, Ill., March 15, 1844

"To the Brethren of the Church of Jesus Christ of Latter

---

* Times and Seasons, vol. 5, p. 423.

Day Saints, living on China Creek, in Hancock County, greeting:—

"Whereas, Brother Richard Hewitt has called on me to-day, to know my views concerning some doctrines that are preached in your place, and states to me that some of your Elders say that a man *having a certain priesthood* may have as many wives as he pleases, and that that doctrine is taught here; I say unto you that man preaches *false doctrine*, for there is no such doctrine taught here, neither is there any such thing practiced here; and any man that is found teaching privately or publicly any such doctrine, is culpable, and will stand a chance of being brought before the High Council, and lose his license and membership also: therefore he had better beware what he is about.

"HYRAM SMITH."*

John Taylor, one of the apostles (who now, by the way, is the husband of six wives), in 1850, only two years before Brigham announced the doctrine, when he admitted that it had been in his possession for some time, and known to such as should know it, declares when on a mission to France very positively against polygamy, as a doctrine not taught or recognized by the church. Mr. Hyde, in his work on the Mormons, says that "Taylor had four wives wrangling and quarrelling at Utah, and was paying attentions to a girl at Jersey, Channel Islands, at the very moment he uttered these wilful, intentional falsehoods!"

In England, the rumor of polygamy being taught in America, endangered the success of the cause in that country, as elsewhere in Europe, when Parley Pratt, to whom I have before referred as being murdered for running off with the wife of another man, thus publicly denounces it in a General Conference of all the European Churches in 1846: "Such a doctrine is not held, known, or practiced as a principle of the Latter Day Saints. *It is but an-*

* Times and Seasons, vol. 5, p. 477.

other name for whoredom, and is as foreign from the real principles of the church as the devil is from God, or as sectarianism is from Christianity."*

Mormonism then is not necessarily polygamy—at least it was not in its early history. The church existed for *twenty years* without the practice being known to the laity as an authorized one, and as I have given the opinions of the most prominent of the clergy on the subject, I propose now to notice how it is treated in their works.

It is a singular fact that the only reference the Mormons make to the Bible as a guide in life, or use its teachings in their arguments, is when they try to defend polygamy. The precedents established by Abraham, David, and Solomon, referred to in the Old Testament, viewed entirely in the abstract, and the pretended revelation to Joseph Smith, are the only authorities claimed for their acts.

Both the Book of Mormon and the Book of Doctrines and Covenants expressly condemn polygamy, and a more positive condemnation of it we could find nowhere. Let the reader judge for himself from the following quotations:—

"And it came to pass that the people of Nephi, under the reign of the second king, began to grow hard in their hearts, and indulged themselves somewhat in wicked practices, such as like unto David of old, desiring many wives and concubines, and also Solomon his son."

"The word of God burdens me because of your grosser crimes. For behold, thus saith the Lord, this people begin to wax in iniquity; they understand not the Scriptures, for they seek to excuse themselves in committing whoredoms, because of the things which were written concerning David, and Solomon his son. Behold David and Solomon truly had many wives and concubines, *Which thing was abominable before me, saith the Lord;* wherefore, thus saith the Lord, I have led this people out of the land of Jerusalem, by the power of mine arm, that I might raise up a righteous branch from the fruits of the loins of Joseph,

* Millennial Star, vol. 6, p. 22.

wherefore, I the Lord God will not suffer that this people shall be like unto them of old. Wherefore, my brethren, hear me, and harken to the word of the Lord, for there shall not any man among you have *save one wife*, and concubines he shall have none, for I, the Lord God, *delighteth in the chastity of women*. And whoredoms are an abomination before me; thus saith the Lord."*

Again:

"Behold the Lamanites, your brethren, whom ye hate because of their filthiness, and the cursing that have come upon their skins, are more righteous than you; for they have not forgotten the commandment of the Lord, which was given unto our fathers, that they should have *save one wife;* and concubines they should have none, and there should not whoredom be committed among them."†

To give force and applicability to these quotations, the teachings of the book, as if to prevent the use of the argument that such teachings were intended only for the nations to whom they were directly given, says that "the Lord speaketh unto one nation like unto another, to prove that he is an unchangeable God."‡

The Book of Doctrines and Covenants the Mormons believe to be as much an inspired work as the Book of Mormon, and to hold to it the same relation that Christians consider the New Testament to have to the Old. This book is equally as explicit on polygamy. It is represented to consist of the later revelations. Hear what it has to say:§

"Thou shalt love *thy wife* with all thy heart, and cleave unto *her* and *none else*, and he that looketh upon a woman to lust after her shall deny the faith, and shall not have the spirit, and if he repents not shall be cast out.||

"And again I say unto you that whoso forbids to marry

---

* Book of Mormon, pp. 116 and 118.
† Ibid. p. 219.
‡ Book of Mormon, p. 107.
§ Book of Mormon, p. 107.
||Book of Doctrines and Covenants, p. 124.

is not ordained of God; for marriage is ordained of God unto man: wherefore it is lawful that he should have *one* wife, and they *twain* shall be one flesh, and all this that the earth might answer the end of its creation, and that it might be filled with the measure of man according to his creation.*

The most remarkable and explicit of all authority on the subject is contained in an appendix to the Book of Doctrines and Covenants, which was published *after the date* of the pretended revelation authorizing polygamy, and the quotation itself purports to be a revelation, strange as it may seem, received about the time of the one entirely contradicting it. It reads as follows:

"Marriage should be celebrated with prayer and thanksgiving, and at the solemnization the persons to be married standing together, etc., he (the person officiating) shall say, calling each by their names, 'you do mutually agree to be each other's companions, husband and wife, observing the legal rights belonging to this condition, that is, keeping yourselves *wholly for each and from all others* during your lives,' and when they shall have answered, 'yes,' he shall pronounce them husband and wife, in the name of the Lord Jesus Christ, by virtue of *the laws of the country* (which prohibit polygamy) and by authority vested in him."

"Inasmuch as this church of Christ has been reproached with the crime of fornication and polygamy, we declare that we believe that *one man should have one wife*, and one woman but one husband, except in case of death, when either is at liberty to marry again."†

I have already quoted from the Book of Mormon to show the universality of the application of its precepts to the whole church. Then we have in their New Testament a passage enjoining obedience to such teachings as *had already* been received, which reads:—

"Thou shalt take the things which thou *hast received*

*Ibid. p. 218.
†Book of Doctrines and Covenants, pp. 330, 331.

which *have been* given unto thee in my scriptures, for a law, to be my law, to govern my church, and he that doeth according to these things shall be saved, and he that doeth them not shall be damned, if he continues."*

The teachings of their scriptures on the subject of polgyamy I have shown to be emphatic. Now let the reader consider these in connection with the late revelation on the subject of polygamy which is too long to be inserted here, but more particularly with the following paragraph in it:

"For all these having this law (the law requiring polygamy) revealed unto them, *must obey the same*, for behold I reveal unto you a new and everlasting covenant, and if ye abide not that covenant ye are damned."

By the Book of Doctrines and Covenants the saints are required to obey its teachings, and those of the Book of Mormon (and these prohibit polygamy), or they will be damned, and by this new revelation they are required to do exactly the opposite, or they will be damned. On this subject they would appear as in a strait betwixt two.

There is another paragraph in this remarkable revelation which must be exceedingly comforting to the married saints, who believe in it as divine, and it is surprising that an unmarried man among the faithful remains in Utah. I suppose, however, it is intended to apply only to those who have duplicated their wives, though by the letter of the revelation, the monogamists may claim its benefits also. It reads as follows:—

"Verily, verily, I say unto you, if a man marry a wife, according to my word, and they are sealed by the Holy Spirit of promise, according to my appointment, *she shall commit any sin or transgression* of the new and everlasting covenant whatever, and all manner of blasphemies, and if he commit no murder, wherein they shed innocent blood, *yet they shall come forth in the first resurrection, and enter into their exaltation*," *etc.*

Here then the saints have a *carte blanche* from the Almighty

---

*Ibid. p. 107.

to become adulterers, rogues, liars, and blasphemers, and finally "enter into their exaltation," upon condition that they will "marry a wife according to covenant." The condition is certainly a very easy one to comply with, as the majority of all Christendom are marrying without expecting any such benefits. The number of each sex in Utah is about equal, and a general application of the revelation, and not confine it to polygamists, would be very effectual, I should think, in stopping the practice, particularly if its benefits were extended to women, who, poor creatures, are dependent upon their husbands for salvation, as they believe.

CHAP. XVI.

PRACTICAL POLYGAMY.

It is far from my purpose to enter into any argument against a practice so unnatural, so degrading, and so abhorrent to the better feelings of the refined of all Christian nations, as polygamy is. Nothing that I might write, in the way of argument, would benefit the masses of this infatuated people, if circulated amongst them, which it never would be; but it is to enlighten the public that they may understand the abominations that exist, that I write. That polygamy was strongly reprehended in the early history of the church they have been taught by some of their own people, who now form the sect of Josephites, and many of the older Mormons knew such to have been the case; but so great is their delusion, that they blindly adhere to the teachings of Brigham Young, however inconsistent they may be.

Motives of policy, combined with a desire for the gratification of the baser passions and lusts, were most unquestionably concerned with the prophet who first authorized and practiced polygamy, and whether that prophet was

Joseph Smith or Brigham Young, it matters not. The existence of the sect seemed to depend upon it. Twenty-one years' experience had settled that question. Proselyting would not make the sect as numerous as the dreams of its founders would have it. Those who became proselytes, through honest motives, were liable to apostatize when they saw their error; but if the church should be built of the progeny of those who remained faithful, their allegiance to it would be stronger. We all know the effect of early education upon the religious status of our lives. Moreover their children could be kept in more complete ignorance of everything outside of Mormonism, which is another desirable consideration. With the impure and lustful, neither such practical arguments as this, or a revelation enjoining it as a duty, with the promise of increased happiness in the eternal world, were necessary to their acceptance of the new doctrine. For society to tolerate their licentiousness was sufficient. But a more powerful influence must operate upon the poor deluded woman to induce her voluntarily to live in a state so unnatural, and so degrading. The revelation meets that end. It both promises reward and threatens punishment. Marriage, by it, is made essential *to happiness in heaven*. It is a part of their theology that an unmarried woman can enter there only in a menial capacity to those more highly favored, and to such it is not even represented as that desirable place which the most contracted views of any Christian would regard it to be.

Celibacy in man is not represented to be so punished, though it is greatly deprecated, and his glory in the eternal world, it is declared, will be proportionate with the number of wives he may have been the means of introducing there, and the number of his children will constitute the size of his eternal kingdom. Hence the importance of multiplying wives.

Not only is increased glory held up to women, who will marry, but to do so is a paramount duty, enjoined by the great head of the Church. Very many simple, confiding, honest women are by such arguments induced to enter into polygamy, and render their lives miserable with the hope of receiving the reward promised for such sacrifices. Is it not natural and beautiful for woman to be influenced by just such motives? The occupants of nuns' cloisters all over Christendom enter their seclusion for the opposite mode of life, with not dissimilar convictions of duty from those which actuate the more sincere of the Mormon women, when they become the second, third or twentieth wife. But in addition to the conviction of duty, and greater security which prompts the nun in her course, the Mormon woman is driven to it as the only possible way of securing the glory to which she aspires.

Upon what other reasonable hypothesis can we account for their acts. Certainly the Mormon woman knows that it is foreign to her nature to be made happy in such relations, and all, of both sexes, who have observed the workings of polygamy, know the tendency is to, and that it *does*, degrade woman. The female Mormon is early taught that she is the inferior of man in everything, and she aspires to be his equal in nothing. She becomes a wife, knowing that she is to be made a servant, rather than a companion and helpmate, and the true relations of the connubial state are entirely perverted.

At present I have no doubt wives become such of their own accord, with the influences to which I have referred operating when such are necessary; but there is pretty strong evidence that in the earlier history of polygamy women were compelled to marry. Judge Cradlebaugh told me that when he was United States Judge in Utah, in 1858, he had the most indisputable evidence that in one of the southern settlements of that territory, on one occasion, forty young girls were confined together in a house, and required to select husbands before they were released. The affidavits of some of them were parts of the evidence.

Affection on the part of man is not made the foundation —the first step toward even a contemplation—of marriage, as it should be, but he enters into it after being somewhat attracted for mere expediency; and not to attribute to him baser motives, which I leave to the imagination of the reader, to discharge what he believes a religious duty, without a thought of the holy and intimate relationship which should exist between husband and wife.

The woman is taken that she may become the mother of his children, and the church benefited by her progeny, and she, from the fact of being a wife, is to have her eternal glory increased. Thus the husband's discharge of duty is also a great act of magnanimity, which is to redound to his future happiness. This is the most favorable construction that can be put on the motives of a Mormon polygamist.

That woman is degraded by polygamy, is a fact of which I have had the most unquestionable evidence, in my own observation, and from the reliable testimony of others, who have had better opportunities of witnessing the practical workings of their iniquitous system.

The polygamous wife of a Mormon is rendered unhappy by all manner of jealousies incident to her life. The piety and affection of a Sarah could not restrain her feelings under such circumstances, and the Mormon wife, with Hagars, and Ishmaels, and Isaacs, often multiplied, could hardly be expected to. But in addition to these natural causes of discontent, arise the unavoidable trials that grow out of her debased situation, in being regarded and treated as the inferior of man—the "weaker vessel" in everything. Abraham loved Sarah, whatever may have been his feelings toward Hagar, but where is the Mormon who really *loves* his wife?

There is a class of "celestial wives," consisting of women who are sealed as spiritual wives for eternity only. They are not supposed to be regarded or treated as wives in this life, but are married to secure to themselves greater happiness in heaven. Brigham Young has a number of this class, in addition to his eighteen or twenty terrestrial wives. The "sealed wives" are to have the same privileges in heaven as if they had been bonâ fide wives on earth. Indeed, unless a wife is sealed to her husband for eternity, she loses all claim to exaltation in glory. Then there is *marrying* for time, and *sealing* for eternity, and either may exist without the other. A woman may have a pretty good fellow for a husband, so far as his social relations with her here are concerned; but she may be a little dubious about his standing in the celestial world, hence she becomes "sealed" to Brigham Young or Heber C. Kimball, or to the late Joseph the Prophet, by getting some one to act as his proxy. Such a course I should think would excite jealousy on the part of the earthly husband, if the man's esteem for his wife (for I cannot admit the existence of a stronger feeling) is sufficient to render him capable of feeling jealous. Only those who are "sealed," I suppose, know all the privileges connected with the relation here, and Mr. Hyde seems to doubt the chastity of such, as he says in his work, "when a woman sinks low enough to prefer another man for her *pseudo*-eternal husband, she is certainly sunk low enough to sin in *deed* as well as in *thought*."

Marriage to a *first* wife is comparatively a very trifling affair, and the ceremony may be performed by an Elder, Deacon, Priest, Bishop, or any other church official—and their name is legion—after a mutual agreement between the interested parties, as in Christian communities. But this is only *marrying*. If the parties wish to be "*sealed*," another, and what is regarded as a more sacred and spiritual service, is required. Formerly this was performed only by the President, and must take place before the altar in the Endowment House. A press of business in that line caused Brigham to delegate to Heber C., his first colleague, this duty.

It is not quite so simple for a saint to become a polygamist as the terrestrial husband of a first wife. The second, and all subsequent marriages, must be performed by the President before the altar. The several necessary preliminary steps are as follows:—

The man must make known to the President his desire to marry a particular lady. Then the President pretends to ascertain the will of God concerning the contemplated marriage. If it is agreeable, the man is then authorized to marry again. Next he communicates with the parents of the lady, and they being willing, he then consults the lady herself. I think if I were a young lady I would prefer taking part a little earlier in the action. The finale of the preliminaries is to obtain the consent of the first wife, when the three go together to the Endowment House, and all participate in the ceremony.

If the first wife withholds her consent, as she has a recognized right to do, the husband may submit the case to the President, when the wife is summoned before him to make known her objections. If they are not strong or tangible, they are overruled as being capricious, and the man is married with the omission of the part provided for the first wife in the ceremony.

Cases sometimes occur where the first wife is capable of interposing very serious obstacles, when the difficulty can be remedied only by divorce, which is easily obtained as I shall hereafter show, or by causing the wife to waive her objections through fear, or because of other influences that may be brought to bear. I will give an example of this kind. A Mormon residing in Salt Lake City, having already one wife, desired to add to the number, and had selected the widow of a brother, who had died a few years before, to share his connubial relations with the other wife. She objected, however, not to his marrying again, but to the woman he wanted to marry, and proved herself to be a good Mormon by offering to select for him another who would be more congenial than the sister-in-law. Rather than submit the case to the President he yielded, and accepted the choice of the wife, a buxom young girl, and soon the three were made one flesh.

But the husband appeared to prefer a particular wife rather than a mere multiplication of them, and the last marriage proved to be rather an unhappy one; he still longed for the brother's widow. The first wife remained inexorable, and as a *dernier resort* he appealed to the president. The wife number one was then brought up to state her objections. She did so in a very business-like or lawyer-like way, and among other things specified that her faith in the doctrine of polygamy was not shaken, for she had only a short time before consented to her husband marrying a second wife, in order that his kingdom might be increased, and would consent to his marrying a third for a similar purpose; but the woman he wished to marry was old, had already been a wife without having borne children, hence the probability was that the great end of marriage, the multiplication of the race, would not be subserved. A more powerful argument could not have been submitted to the president, and he dare not overrule it (if he dared not do anything). The Saint was a friend of Brigham, and he wanted to accommodate him, therefore he divorced the two wives the man had already, and married him to the woman of his choice. *

Polygamy in its best phases and surroundings is bad enough, but the marrying of relatives and incest as practised in Utah is most abominable and disgraceful.

Marrying several members of the same family relationship is by no means uncommon. For several sisters to be wives of one man, and mothers and daughters also, are of frequent occurrences. One of the principal merchants of Salt Lake City married three sisters all of whom are still living. But one of the most disgraceful cases of incest I have seen recorded was the marriage of a well known individual to his *half sister*. This is an indisputable fact. She lived in her brother's family for several months, generally regarded as one of the wives of Brigham Young, but when about giving birth to her first child she announced to her brother's other wives (for he had two others) that he was

---

* In this case, as in all others that I may cite in illustration of the customs and lives of the Mormons, I have the names of the parties referred to; but as the mention of them in no instance would add to the interest of the narrative, and in some cases would cause an unwarranted mortification to friends of the parties, whom I respect, if these letters should fall into their hands, I withhold them.

the father of her child, the announcement quite surprised the household, as well as the community, and was for a time the subject of gossip, but as the woman had been married by the president it was regarded as above suspicion of wrong. For several years she continued to live with her half-brother bearing other children by him, and no effort was then made to conceal the double relationship. Her mother was also the mother of her husband, living in the family; and finally her treatment by her brother-husband became so cruel that she left his house and sought refuge at Camp Douglas, and afterward with her mother went back to the States with a company of Josephites. Another shocking feature in this case was the brother and husband's charge of a want of chastity in her relations to other men.

I know of one instance of a Mormon proposing to marry a widow lady, her daughter of sixteen, and a woman she had as a servant, and to bind himself to marry a younger daughter as soon as she was of marriageable age. The proposition being declined, he made a bold attempt to obtain the servant alone; but he failed in this also, not without making a rather unusual effort however, and the *dernier resort*, which terminated his unsuccessful suit, was the promise that if the woman would have him he would give her the best hog in his stye, which she might sell, and use the money as she pleased. Here is an example for the benefit of young ladies in the States as to the appreciation of their sex in Utah, one of them being regarded as about the equivalent of a hog. The individual was about sixty years of age, and had a son of twenty, who subsequently sought and obtained the hand of the maid. Taking the father's age as the maximum of marriageable years, while the minimum is fourteen for girls, and sixteen for boys, we have quite a long period when parties are in the market as husbands or wives.

As I have before remarked, the women are not required to marry a particular individual, or indeed to marry at all, if they are willing to risk the consequences; but they are often "counselled" to do so. The influence of counsel the Mormons too well understand. With the more timid it amounts to a command. An intelligent lady who was a member of the Mormon church until she became disgusted with its abominations, informed me that four years ago she was repeatedly "counselled" to marry against her wishes, and on more than one occasion her bishop had been so kind as to name the individual he "counselled" her to marry.

I have heard of one instance of the man and woman both being required to marry, on the grounds that they had previously agreed to do so, and afterwards flew the track. A saint who had one wife already, was attracted by a young woman in Liverpool, when on a mission there, and promised to marry her; but it could not be consummated in England, where the laws against bigamy are rigidly enforced, and as they had to be separated, the man placed to the credit of the woman in the emigration office the cost of her transportation to Salt Lake. For some cause she did not come over that year, but came afterwards. Time and distance has a wonderful effect in cooling the ardor of lovers, and when there is no love, but only attraction, indifference is likely soon to result. Such was the case with our Elder and his espoused, and by mutual consent the match was regarded as broken. Some time afterwards Brigham learned of the circumstances, and the woman was *required* to become the third wife of the former missionary. I did not learn of any criminal intimacy existing to cause the compulsory marriage, which indeed was as much so on one party as on the other.

It is not uncommon for a woman, who is the lawful wife of a Gentile, to leave her husband, and live as a wife of a Mormon. Brigham Young has a woman in his harem who is the wife of a gentleman in Boston, and Parley Pratt, once one of the most prominent apostles, was shot and killed by an enraged husband for taking his wife from California to Salt Lake City, and there marrying her. The little boy who brought me fresh water to wash the briny solution from my body, at the time of my bath in the lake, spoke very affectionately of his father in New Jersey, when his mother was living with a man in Salt Lake city. Such cases are numerous.

Bishops are often appealed to by men and women to obtain for them husbands or wives, and they are exceedingly accommodating in this way. The official will undertake the task, and go to work in as business-like way as he would to negotiate a loan, and perhaps bring the parties together, on the occasion of the marriage ceremony, for the first time in their lives. I think if I were a Mormon I would about as soon advertise in the New York *Herald.*

I recently heard of a rather hurried union that took place a few years ago in high life in the metropolis of Mormondom. One evening, at the house of a prominent man in the church, a small company had assembled, including his son and quite an estimable young lady. After tea, the two happened to be sitting together on a sofa, when the thoughtful parent approached, and in a very blunt way, as he is in the habit of doing things, remarked, "Well, William, Mary is a good girl and will make you a good wife;" and to Mary he said, "Now Mary, you can't find a better man for a husband than William; so stand up here, both of you, and let me marry you." The lady was quite shocked, and at first demurred; but after a little conversation between the interested, they concluded that the father was the best judge in such matters, and when the company separated that evening they were man and wife.

Those who are familiar with the cost of a lady's wardrobe in New York, and other incidental expenses attending their movements in society, may suppose that with the more prominent and wealthy Mormons at least, the expense of keeping several women in a way to sustain the position they hold, would be considerable; but such is by no means the case. The very large majority of Mormon wives are self-supporting, and required to be so. There is an exception in the household of the President. His wives and daughters are not required to labor to earn money, but they attend to all their domestic concerns, and weave cloth for their own use, which duties are quite sufficient to keep in their minds a lively sense of their subordination, and at the same time save their husband and father numerous little millinery and dress-making bills, servants' wages, etc.

With the families of most other church officials it is different. The wives of the second President, Mr. Kimball, are publicly known as dress-makers, milliners, etc., and the elder of them openly speak of having been no expense to their husbands since they left Nauvoo. That the wives of the apostles labor for what they can earn I have evidence in a pair of gloves one of them made for me, and she seemed very glad to accept the patronage of a Gentile, though the President is decidedly opposed to reciprocating such business transactions, and cautions his people against trading with Gentiles.

The majority of polygamists furnish their wives with certain necessary articles, such as rations of flour and meat, with wood, house-room and shoes, and they are expected to purchase with their own earnings all additional articles. They spin and weave their own cloth. A laboring man will, if possible, have a Danish woman as one of his wives, as they are usually good weavers, and can assist the others in making their cloth, etc.

So it may be inferred that polygamy, under the Brigham Young regimé is not necessarily an expensive institution Indeed if a man has three or four thrifty women to work for him he may find them pecuniarily profitable.

Very many of the women who marry polygamists accept their state from the beginning as a necessary trial, and enter it with a very commendable Christian fortitude, determined to bear their afflictions for the glory that is to follow. Mr. Bowles, in his work "Across the Continent," remarks that he met a sweet, gentle, amiable woman, with whom he conversed about her life as one of the wives of a polygamist, when she remarked, "That the Lord Jesus has laid a great trial on me, but I mean to bear it for His sake, and for the glory He will give me in His kingdom." What beautiful Christian sentiment is contained in the remark of this poor, misguided, but sincere woman. More highly favored Christians might learn a lesson of true piety and resignation from it.

How numerous this class of women are I can form no idea. It is rarely the case that one is so situated that she dare converse on the subject with a Gentile. Such meekness, I imagine, is not the rule, and only here and there you find those sweet, simple, amiable dispositions, that are more divine than human, whether in an honest member of a corrupt sect, or the angel-like wife of a Christian missionary doing good to the destitute and suffering around her. The tendency of Mormonism without polygamy is not to encourage such piety, and with polygamy it is to root it out, and even destroy the natural gentler traits of character.

Jealousy is the one great cause of unhappiness among the wives of a polygamist. There are other incidental causes constantly arising, sufficient in themselves to mar the happiness of an angel on earth, but jealousy is the worm that gnaws at the vitals of their social life. Often it exists to such an extent that the several wives of a Mormon have to be furnished separate quarters, and in some instances they are furnished homes in different parts of the country. One individual I know has his wives separated about thirty miles, and another keeps one wife eighty miles from the other four. Mr. Greeley mentions, in his lecture on the Mormons, one family where two or more wives lived together in the same house, and would not speak to each other.

The first wife is almost universally regarded by the husband with more favor than the others, which immediately gives rise to that dreaded passion, and at an early day she secures the ill-will of her "sisters." This favoritism may be observed in Brigham's conduct toward Amelia, his last wife, and from him down through all the gradations of polygamists. The first wife, more than intermediate ones, is jealous of attentions to the last; but in this respect there is no great difference between them, they all unite in the feeling. A lady not long ago informed me that she had visited a house in the city where there were three wives. The husband was absent at the time, and the three together entertained her apparently very harmoniously, but when the husband came in, the last wife, certainly in bad taste, went and sat on his knee. This so displeased the others, that they immediately left the room with their guest sitting there.

It is not uncommon for a second, third or fourth wife to be confined in child-bed, without the first manifesting the slightest interest in her case. At first blush it may seem very unnatural for a woman to be devoid of sympathy under such circumstances. But it must also be unnatural for her to feel much pleased when she considers the fact of her husband being the father of a child which is not her own.

The unpleasant feeling existing between wives is not confined to them, but a want of congeniality between husband and wife is most marked. This naturally grows out of the degradation in which woman is held, to which I have before alluded. The belief in their systems, whether a man becomes a polygamist or not, is almost certain to result in improper treatment of his wife, as he is taught to regard woman in a very different light from that in which she is regarded in Christian communities. I know of one case where this change took place. An *intelligent* man who became a Mormon after having lived many years as an affectionate and indulgent husband, always conferring with his wife in all his plans in life, and I have no doubt profiting by her advice. They were English, and in Liverpool he associated a good deal with the clergy, and through them was led to a change in his views, as to the relation that should exist between husband and wife. Accordingly, one day he instructed the wife as to how she should act in the future. She was not to presume, thereafter, to advise or counsel him in anything, nor even suggest a thing that might influence his judgment; particularly if she held different views from himself; that if he should contemplate marrying other women she was not to oppose him in any way., but quietly to submit. This was exactly the opposite to what he seemed to desire up to the moment of the conversation, and the change was to be as sudden as it was radical.

I have before spoken of the resignation and submission with which wives accept their lot, and of the causes of their unhappiness, but it is not common for them to admit that polygamy is the real cause of their discontent. I cited one case where the woman was willing to submit to it all in a good Christian spirit; but occasionally one is found who talks plainly of her situation. One of the wives of an apostle has frequently been heard to reproach herself for present unhappiness. She recently remarked to a friend "If I had not been the *thing* I was, to marry as I did, I would not be so unhappy now; but I have no one but myself to blame, I did it all." This same lady is often emphatic in her injunctions to her daughter, in the presence of others, never to marry until she is sure of having a husband of *her own.* This class I have no doubt is more numerous than the one I referred to elsewhere.

A Mormon wife who does not become a mother within a reasonable time after marriage, suffers in the estimation in which she is held by the Saints generally, and if she should happen to have a second husband and still no issue she is almost despised by her sex. This, however, does not apply to Amelia, the last wife of Brigham, who has been married two or three years, as her unfruitfulness may be accounted for from natural causes.

The tendency of polygamy being to immorality generally, I might refer to indecency in conversation as particularly observed. This occurs with women and children as well as men. Several wives of one man, with their children present, have been known to indulge in such indecent conversation as would bring the blush to the face of a modest woman if repeated to her alone. The result of this may be seen in the precociousness of their children in certain ways. Urchins of eight or nine, know more of what they should not know, than youths of sixteen or eighteen in a refined community. They are not only afforded opportunities of thus corrupting their minds, but often encouraged to do so.

CHAPTER XVII

POLYGAMY CONTINUED.

That the wives of polygamists in Utah are unhappy and discontented I have already endeavored to show, and it is a fact patent to all who have observed them. But the reader will be somewhat surprised to learn that discontent and "whining," as it is called, existed, even in the harem of the Prophet, as long ago as 1856. That such was the case Brigham Young admitted in a sermon preached in the tabernacle that year for the special benefit of the women. Polygamy among them—that is among all but the few that had been favored, was in its infancy; but the little leaven of discontent existing then, even in high places, has been going on leavening the whole. Brigham's plain talk on this occasion was as follows:

"Now for my proposition. It is more particularly for the sisters, as it is frequently happening that women say they are unhappy. Men will say: 'My wife, though a most excellent woman, has not seen a happy day since I took my second wife.' 'No, not a happy day for a year,' says one; and another has not seen a happy day for five years (and such must have been among the clandestine wives of polygamists, for it had not been published as a doctrine of the church but four years before). It is said that women are tied down and abused, that they are misused, and that they are wading through a perfect flood of tears because of the folly of some men as well as their own folly.

"I wish *my women* (Heber Kimball sometimes calls his wives his *cows*,) to understand that what I am going to say is for them as well as others, and I want those that are here to tell their sisters—yes, all the women in the country—and then write it back to the States, and do as you please with it. I am going to give you from this time to the 6th day of October next (the day the semi-annual conference was to meet) for reflection, that you may determine whether you wish to stay with your husbands or not; and then I am going *to set every woman at liberty*, and say to them: 'Now, go your way. My own women with the rest, *go your way*.' And my wives have got to do one of two things—either round up their shoulders and endure the afflictions of this world, and love their religion, or they may leave, for I will not have them about me. I will go into heaven alone rather than have scratching and fighting around me. *I will set all at liberty*. What, first wife too? Yes, I will liberate you all. I know what my women will say: 'You may have as many wives as you please, Brigham.' (That is rather inconsistent with their scratching and fighting around him). 'But I want to go somewhere, or do something, to get rid of these whiners."* The thing to be done, I would respectfully suggest, would be to give up his iniquitous system of polygamy.

With this want of congeniality and harmony in the family of the Prophet, who is considered so desirable as a husband, that a woman once, Jacob-like, served seven years as a domestic in his family, that she might at the end of her servitude become one of his wives, what must have been the state of domestic affairs in the families of those less highly favored?

The offer of Brigham, to those who are unacquainted with Mormon fanaticism, and their surroundings, and circumstances in life, might appear as a very liberal one to the discontented. But it was really a taunt, as unkind as their escape, if they desired it, was impracticable. While they

* Deseret *News*, Oct. 1st, 1856.

whined, and scratched, and fought, they still regarded their sufferings as necessary. They were "enduring the afflictions of this world." But suppose they desired to avail themselves of the offer? They must leave behind their children, which to all mothers would be a sore trial. And how would they "go their way," and whither would they go? There was a population of Mormons only in the territory, and they would not assist them. There were no United States troops as now. It was more than a thousand miles to civilization, and they had no means to obtain transportation, for they were penniless. There was a tall range of mountains, almost impassable in the winter, which would have prevented a journey in private conveyances or on foot, but their destitute condition would have made such a journey as impracticable as any other. But supposing the possibility of overcoming these obstacles, what awaited them in a Christian community? They had degraded themselves, unwittingly it is true, but still degraded in the light of Christianity, or even civilization. Some provision would have been made for such, of course, but they would naturally shrink from the encounter.

Then, if they had accepted the offer with the hope of remaining in the valley, how would they have been treated? It is doubtful if they would be allowed to remain at all, for they were told to "go," and their influence would have been bad on others if they remained; and the fanaticisim of the people would have been so increased that thay would have been regarded as outcasts, most debased, in the eyes of their persecutors.

The sermon had its desired effect to some extent I have no doubt, not because of its liberality, but, on the contrary, by more deeply crushing the spirits of the unhappy women. They had declined the alternative, then they must "round up their shoulders" and "endure the afflictions," be they increased as they might. Brigham Young's seeming clemency was but another politic act of despotism.

After what I have written about marriage relation—how it is entered into and how regarded—it will not be surprising to any one to learn that divorces are numerous. They are granted by the President for very trival causes. Sometimes upon mutual agreement; oftener upon the application of the interested, who may have been aggrieved, or imagined they have. When the application proceeds from a woman it may be set down as a rule that it is from good cause. I was rather surprised to learn that the wishes of a woman would be considered at all; but if she has evidence to present of neglect of her husband, or of his unkind treatment of her, and there is a probability of her marrying again, the divorce will almost certainly be forthcoming. This is more particularly the case with the poorer classes. With the more influential the wishes of the husband would receive very grave consideration. From what I have alreadv said about women being taught that marriage is so essential to their future glory, it might be supposed that their belief in this respect would prevent them from applying for divorce, but such an application is by no means evidence of scepticism. The woman knows too well what a marketable commodity she is, and almost any of them would be willing to risk the chances of getting other men to introduce them into heaven if they desired a change of the relations of this life. There is not the slightest objection to a divorced woman marrying again; she is supposed to hold the same relation to society as if her husband were dead; and, indeed, she is "counselled" to take another. The laws of marriage and divorce are so lightly considered that a Bishop not long since, when addressing his sisters in a ward meeting, remarked: "If your husband doesn't suit you put *him* away and take another," and repeated the changes until he had provided the seventh husband, if so many trials should be necessary before a suitable one was found. I suppose his advice to the other sex would be "if your first wife doesn't suit you, take another, and if she should not, another and another *ad infinitum*, omiting the 'put her away.'" That is, he must keep them all.

Mr. Hyde says he knew a woman in Salt Lake City who had been married six times (she was then one short of the

Bishop's limit), and that *four* of her previous husbands were then living in the city. Ten years have passed since Mr. Hyde wrote, and she may have still further multiplied her divorces at this date.

Frequent application for divorce, for the most trivial imaginary causes had so annoyed the President that he determined upon a plan to diminish the number, and at the same time add to the receipts of his office. Of this Mr. Hyde speaks as follows:—

"So common did the applications for divorce become, that in 1854, Brigham had to impose a price to be paid in cash (*then very scarce*) upon all bills. He charged ten dollars if married for time, and fifty dollars if sealed for eternity. The money went mostly to the clerk. Not a few amusing scenes occurred where parties who came for divorces had to return and live together because they could not raise money enough between them to pay for the 'bill.' It had the desired effect; it decreased the applications."

When a Mormon woman marries a Gentile, and becomes dissatisfied with her new lord, even though she has violated the law of the church, and may have been cut off from fellowship with the Saints, a divorce is readily obtained upon the slightest pretext. I know of two instances of this kind where divorces were granted for desertion of the husbands, when they were only temporarily absent, and one of them for a few days, at Fort Bridger. The husbands suspected nothing when they left, and returned rather surprised to find their former spouses joined to others. One of the husbands was an upright, intelligent and very worthy young man, who had been married but a short time. From what I learned of the character of the woman, he might congratulate himself in getting rid of her as he did.

As a result of their "peculiar institution," I believe that adultery is more common among the Mormons than any class of people in the country, since the suppression of free-love societies. This may be regarded as a very bold declaration in the face of their assumed unexampled virtue. Public prostitution, does not exist in the territory, and to this the Mormon points so triumphantly as evidence of virtue. But if they are a virtuous people, even admitting those living in polygamy to be, it must be from some differently understood meaning of the word from that as usually conceded when referring to the relations between the sexes. How they reconcile their acts with their teaching, that adultery is a mortal sin that can be atoned for only by the shedding of blood, is a mystery which I can solve only upon the supposition that sin is not imputed to them as *sin*. I have information, from what I consider very reliable authority, of the practice of adultery by men well known in the church, both at home and abroad, when on missions preaching Mormonism. For children to be born in the household of an absent brother who may have been years away on a mission is considered a fortunate circumstance for the absent one, as his kingdom in the eternal world is thus increased. I am told that such is of frequent occurrence among the more vulgar and honest. What all Christianity would regard as sinful and criminal, I must infer is considered a Christian duty by the saints!

Polygamy in Salt Lake City, has extended its baneful influences throughout the adjacent country, outside the pale of the church. I have never visited a locality where women so little regard virtue, and men are so devoid of a sense of honor in their relations to the other sex, as in Utah. This is frequently spoken of by the Mormons, who make invidious comparisons between their people and Gentiles in this respect—referring to the outer life of the two classes. They fail to see all this immorality as the fruits of their iniquitous system.

Large numbers of soldiers, and others, thrown into this country during the last four years, and cut off from the restraining influences of home associations, are here exposed to the corrupt ones every where existing, and are morally ruined.

While I admit the absence of public prostitution in Salt Lake City, I must assert its existence, in another form, among women whose ideas of morality and virtue have been so completely perverted, that they willingly embrace opportunities of becoming mistresses of Gentiles. Whether these are of a class who, in all honesty, once accepted the common infatuation, and have had their eyes open to see their real condition as others see it, and are willing to accept *any* degradation, rather than remain where they were; or whether they are women fallen as other women have, I am unable to say. In either case there is no doubt of the state of society among the Mormons leading to their ruin.

When the California and Nevada volunteers returned home, at the close of the war, numbers of Mormon women accompanied the soldiers. Some of them were married by Judges of the United States Courts, and both husbands and wives acted in good faith, and may make honorable members of society; others were married by adjutants of regiments, and the ceremony, altogether illegal, only intended as a farce; while others went off together without desiring to be considered husband and wife, bold and shameless in their adultery.

Polygamy has probably reached its critical stage among the Mormons of Utah. The multiplication of wives is not going on as before. The Act of Congress making it criminal has, probably, to some extent, prevented an increase of the evil, while it has not remedied it. That it has changed the opinions of the people as to their *right* to be polygamists as long as it is sanctioned by the church, I do not believe, though they may not consider it as *expedient* to be. It has probably aroused a little healthful fear. General Babcock in his report of an inspection tour through Utah, last summer, mentions that he learned from Judge Titus, the Chief Justice of the territory, that since the passage of the Act of Congress prohibiting polygamy, some of the Mormons have already put away their unlawful wives, and others declined to become polygamists. Such cases, however, I am inclined to think are very uncommon. Whether from a declining popularity, and threatening failure of this darling doctrine of the leaders, or not, I am unable to say, but polygamy is more strongly advocated now than ever before, and though some may be putting away their unlawful wives, and others refuse to become polygamists, it is as popular in high places as ever. Only a few days before the date of this writing a considerable excitement arose in Zion because a young daughter of the editor of *The Telegraph*, sixteen years old, was married as the fourth wife of a son of the president, while the principal merchant of the city had previously applied to her father for her as his fourth wife, and was refused.

Brigham Young would make it appear that he is more strongly impressed as to the propriety of polygamy than he ever was before. At the last semi-annual conference when a large congregation of people from the rural districts was assembled he made this a special subject. These people know but little of how polygamy is regarded out of Utah, and are a class who regard their prophet as next in wisdom to the Omniscient, hence his desire to impress strongly upon them, their duties and privileges in this respect. On the occasion referred to, he addressed them as follows:

"The last time I was in the City of Lowell there were fourteen thousand more females than males in that one city. This was many years ago. They live and die in a single state, and are forgotten. Have they filled the measures of their creation, and accomplished the design of heaven in bringing them upon the earth? No, they have not. Two thousand good, God-fearing men should go there, and take to themselves seven wives apiece. It is written in the Bible, 'and in that day, seven women shall lay hold of one man, saying, we will eat our bread and wear our own apparel; only let us be called by thy name, to take away our reproach.' The government of the United States does not intend that that prophecy shall be fulfilled, and the Lord Almighty means that it shall.

"Do you not think that the Lord will conquer? I think He will, and we are helping Him. It is the decree of the Almighty that in the last days seven women shall take hold of one man, etc., to be counseled and advised by him, being willing to spin their own clothing, and do everything they can to earn their own living, if they can only bear his name to take away their reproach. What is this order for? It is for the resurrection; it is not for this world. I would not go across this Bowery for polygamy, if it only pertained to this world. It is for the resurrection; and the Spirit of the Lord has come upon the people, and upon the ladies especially, and prepares the way for the fulfillment of His Word. The female sex have been deceived so long, and been troddeen under foot of man so long, that a spirit has come upon them, and they want a place, and a name, and a head; for the man is the head of the woman, to lead her into the celestial kingdom of our Father and God."*

During the past winter the Salt Lake *Telegraph* has abounded with editorials in defence of polygamy as never before. It would make it appear as vital to their religion as the doctrine of the atonement, or of the resurrection. For days in succession long double-leaded editorial articles on this subject have been published. The following has been given as examples: It was the daughter of this writer who the other day was married into the Young family:

" * * However, as to the question, cannot our citizens renounce polygamy? It is just the same sort of question as might have been put to Gallileo, would he not renounce the theory about the earth turning round the sun? Or the ancient Apostles, could they not renounce their doctrine concerning the Redeemer, lowly born, crucified and risen? Or any other apostle of religious, scientific or other class of truths, could they not renounce their favorite theories? Could not Franklin renounce his electricity theories, or Watt his steam theories?

* * * * * * * * *

"Polygamy is not dependent on the Mormons, nor are they upon it. It is not responsible for them nor they for it. The system of plural marriage is a Divine institution, a true and life-giving system, made known from the heavens, and practised by the people of God, as well as those who know

---

* Deseret *News*, October, 1866.

nothing of Him, for thousands upon thousands of years. Faith in the principle and the practice of it when and where necessary, are just as incumbent on the people as faith in and the practice of any other divine truth. The rejection of one truth is sin, just as much as the rejection of another.

"So far as the people of this territory are concerned, they believe and practice polygamy not because any other people did or do, or did not or do not the same thing, but because it is a part of the law of God to them. If the great Jehovah were to make known to them that He wished them to discontinue the practice of polygamy, those of our citizens who are now foremost in the observance of this doctrine would, with corresponding alacrity and faithfulness, cease to observe it, but until such shall be the case, they cannot relinquish the doctrine and remain acceptable before God.

"Let us ask our friends how they would regard our people, if they, convinced that polygamy were a part of the law of God incumbent on them, were to weekly renounce it through fear of the threatenings of puny man, and most all of such specimens of the race as many politicians are? What account of their stewardships could our people render to their Father in Heaven, if they were to abandon His truths at every breath of powerful or popular disfavor? They would be unworthy of the regard or esteem of either God or man. Better, far better, for them to abide in God's truths and risk the consequences. By so doing they will win and retain the favor of heaven, and the fellowship of the illustrious and worthy of our race in all ages, and having the blessings secure, they can afford to risk the bad will and vaporous threatenings of the rest of mankind."

Let me caution my Massachusetts friends *before* they read the following not to get up a female emigration society to Utah, after they learn the advantages of polygamy to women as taught by the Mormons, for it might not prove a more successful one than the famous Washington Territory enterprise:

"Are the wives of polygamists injured? Wherein are they

hurt? Have they not the same privilege of being respected as honorable wives and mothers as any other women have? It is their own free will and choice to become wives of polygamists, and why should they complain of having their own way? For our part we think polygamy is a mighty fine thing for the women, and we will tell you why. In the first place it insures every woman a husband, which monogamy does not; in the second place it gives them the privilege of getting a good husband, which monogamy frequently does not, the latter system granting to many only Hobson's choice; in the third place, it gives a woman the privilege of having the man whom she would prefer of all others, if she can persuade him, and monogamy often prevents such a desirable consummation. How, therefore, the women who are married to polygamists can be injured by it we cannot conceive."*

In addition to the influence of the pulpit and press, the Legistature of the Territory, in its official capacity, comes to the relief of polygamy. On the 13th of January they adopted a memorial to Congress, setting forth in a long preamble the wrongs that have been done the people of Utah by the act of Congress of 1862 prohibiting polygamy, and claiming its repeal on the ground of its unconstitutionality, etc. No one knows better than Brigham Young the utter uselessness of such a memorial. But all such acts have their effects upon this fanatical people.† The result of this petition in the House of Representatives was the adoption of a report declaring polygamy to be a relic of heathenism and barbarism, and but prostitution by another name, and making it obligatory upon officers of the Government to rigidly enforce existing laws on the subject.

Place these remarks alongside of such passages as I have quoted in a previous letter, and compare their teachings of to-day on the subject of marriage with the teachings of 1850, and can a sect so inconsistent, if there were not other things

---

* Salt Lake *Telegraph*, Jan. 29, 1867.
† Ibid. Jan. 31, 1867.

pointing to its end, be expected long to exist. This effort of the pulpit, press and legislature to bolster up the church may be a *dernier resort* when they see ruin impending. Those specially urgent in the maintenance of the "institution" have their "entangling alliances" therewith, and it is but natural that they should act as they do. The cloud they see rising in the church has already reached dimensions larger than a man's hand, and will rise as certainly as did Elijah's, and soon be pouring out in this case its destructive element.

Intestine trouble is likely to arise from incredulity as to the correctness of doctrine and practice; and if skepticism should spread as to the truth of the doctrines of polygamy, it would not only endanger the standing of Brigham and his polygamists, but seal for ever the fate of the sect. A rigid enforcement of law would only increase the fanaticism of the people, which they would construe to be persecution for religious opinions, and would bind them the more strongly together; but a growing unbelief in and abandonment of polygamy, without it being renounced by authority, would knock out the keystone of the arch, and the whole superstructure of Mormonism would fall.

Polygamy is not so general in Utah as many suppose. There are probably more polygamists in Salt Lake City and the Bishops of the settlements than in the whole of the territory besides. The number of women, probably, very slightly exceeds the number of men in Utah. In 1860, there were 20,178 men and 19,947 women, but the proportion has been increased in favor of the women since that time. The very large majority of these are wives of monogamists; and when we consider the number in the harems of the prominent in Salt Lake City and other large settlements, it leaves not very many who can be polygamists, even supposing there is a preponderance in favor of the men among the unmarried.

Having so many in the church who are not restrained in their religious views by selfish considerations, and with a schism already, and with all the Christian world discountenancing polygamy, is there not danger? I think Brigham Young and his satellites fully realize it. The Gentile population is increasing both in the city, and elsewhere, notwithstanding Brigham's efforts to prevent it, by refusing to sell or rent property to such, and by discouraging all business patronage of them. The railroad is approaching Zion from both the Atlantic and Pacific. When completed, a flood of Gentiles will be poured into, and through the territory, mingling more or less with the masses of the people.

The Mormons dare not institute polygamy, until far away from civilization, though they claimed to have had divine authority long before. An evil, then, which would not be tolerated in the States, before the existence of a law forbidding it, because of the abhorrence with which it would have been regarded by the people, (though it existed clandestinely) cannot much longer be tolerated within the jurisdiction of the government, and its statute-books disgraced by a law, when no effort is made to enforce it, though violated every day. That some active measures must be adopted speedily, is evident, unless the Prophet has a revelation for himself and people to shake the dust of this wicked country from their feet, and tread upon its soil no more for ever. This would be a most happy solution of the difficulty attending an abolition of the practice of polygamy. Now the law is not only violated, but publicly ridiculed by the highest authority of the church. Brigham has frequently remarked in the Tabernacle that he "wouldn't give a d——n for a woman who wasn't worth more to a man than five hundred dollars"—the penalty for the first violation of the law. I might here explain that Brigham represents that all his swearing is done in the pulpit. The Prophet has himself violated the law at least once by marrying Amelia.

The following account of an interview between Mr. Colfax and his associates and Brigham Young, is evidence that the Prophet's mind is not altogether at ease on this subject:—

"In the course of the discussion, Mr. Young asked, 'suppose polygamy is given up, will not your government then demand more—will it not war upon the Book of Mormon, and attack our church organization?' The reply was emphatically 'No,' that it had no right, and could have no justification to do so, and that we had no idea that there would be any disposition in that direction.

"The talk which was said to be the freest and frankest ever known on that subject, in that presence, ended pleasantly, but with the full expression on the part of Mr. Colfax and his friends that the polygamy question might be removed from existence, and thus all objection to the admission of Utah as a State taken away; but that until it was, no such admission was possible, and that the government could not continue to look indifferently upon the enlargement of so offensive a practice. And not only what Mr. Young said, but his whole manner, left us the impression that if public opinion and the government united vigorously, but at the same time discreetly, to press the question, there would be found some way to acquiesce in the demand, and change the practice of the present fathers of the church."*

Such admissions. under such circumstances, are significant, but they would not be made publicly, for the people's faith would be shaken. The President would talk so before them. But Brigham Young is a profound diplomatist, in his way, and with the example of Joseph Smith, and others, who publicly denounced polygamy, while they were privately practising it, what would there be to surprise the public in Brigham's course should a way yet be found to discontinue it, in the face of what is now transpiring. The Mormons are a people of contradictions and inconsistencies.

I have dwelt thus freely upon the peculiar institution of Mormonism, because it is the only thing connected with the church that is of special interest to the public, either because of its vice or virtue, and if the government institute hostile measures against the Mormons it will be solely for this cause, and to rid the country of so foul a blot on her his-

---

*Across the Continent. Bowles. Page 112.

tory. How we may peaceably remove this disgrace I will make the subject of some concluding remarks in another chapter.

CHAPTER XVIII.

WHERE THE MORMONS COME FROM, AND HOW THEY REACH SALT LAKE.

In almost every country where the Protestant churches of Great Britain and the United States have their missionaries, there may also be found the preachers of Mormonism sent out from the Valley of the Great Salt Lake.

The earnestness and enthusiasm of this infatuated people in their missionary labor, when viewed in the abstract, must command universal admiration. That their sect should increase in numbers from year to year under their missionary system among the classes that compose the proselytes is not surprising; nor is it surprising that the corrupt church holds within her walls so many of her converts when we consider all the circumstances in the case: the class of people; their delusion, and how they are isolated in Utah with all avenues to their enlightenment closed.

Nineteen-twentieths of the additions to the Mormons that take place from year to year, are from the most degraded of the peasantry of Europe, while Great Britain probably furnishes three times as many as all of the rest of the world (including our country) combined. The following statement of the emigration to Utah for several years, is obtained from the work of Captain Burton on the Mormons. This writer possessed remarkable facilities for obtaining correct information from their records. For weeks he was a constant visitor at the historian's office in Salt Lake City; besides having the confidence of their prominent men, he through them learned much of their history, which he has given to the public in his elaborate work the "City of the Saints," carefully avoiding, however, all unfavorable allusion that it was possible to avoid. About emigration he says:—

"I now proceed to figures, which can easily be verified by reference to Liverpool. From 1840 to 1854 they reckoned seventeen thousand one hundred and ninety-five souls, and from 1854 to 1855, four thousand seven hundred and sixteen souls, the total in fifteen years (1840-'55) being twenty-one thousand nine hundred and eleven. From 1855 to 1856 they number four thousand three hundred and ninety-five souls, and from the 1st of July 1857 to 30th of June 1860, they count two thousand four hundred and thirty-three, making for the five subsequent years (1855-'60) a total of six thousand eight hundred and twenty-eight. Thus in twenty years between 1840-'60 they show a grand total of twenty-eight thousand seven hundred and thirty-nine immigrants."

I have already said that three-fourths of this immigration was from Great Britain, and give as an example the nationalities of the people that arrived between the years 1857-'60 as recorded by the same writer:—"From the United Kingdom of Great Britain and Ireland—English, one thousand and seventy-four; Scotch one hundred and twenty-six; Welsh one hundred and seventy-three; Irish twelve. The total number from the Scandinavian missions is seven hundred and sixty-two, of which there are five hundred and twenty-eight Danes, one hundred and ninety-three Swedes, and forty-one Norwegians. The total number from the Swiss and Italian missions is two hundred and eleven, of which two hundred and nine are from the Swiss Cantons, and two from Italy. There are also two French, and three Germans, and seventy Elders returning home from missions, making a grand total of two thousand four hundred and thirty-three." Since 1860 other missions have been established in addition to those reported above.

I will now endeavor to explain the workings of their missionary and emigration systems, which add so many to the population of Utah every year. Proselyting and emigration go together. When an individual accepts their religious creed, and joins the church, he is taught that it is his duty, and will greatly conduce to his happiness to emigrate immediately to Zion in America.

At the April session of the semi-annual conferences, in Salt Lake City, the elective officers of the church are elected, and the appointments of others announced. Among the latter are the appointments to missions. A man must have been ordained an Elder, before he is eligible to the office of a missionary, and the more important missions are supplied by persons ranking high among the clergy. The English mission is considered the most desirable, and is usually filled by one of the Twelve. The head of the mission is called the president. The president has two counsellors, also of high grade. He might be said to control all foreign missions, as his duties pertain to other works, as well as that over which he more immediately presides.

For labor among the people Elders are sent out, subject to the orders of the president, and are responsible to him for the manner in which they discharge their duties. They usually go in pairs; but larger numbers are sent to the more important missions, and the largest to the English, as might be inferred from the statistics of emigration.

All missionary appointments are made by the president of the church, and announced at the conclusion of the conference, just as are the appointments of ministers to their stations, by the annual conferences of the Methodist church. Usually it is understood beforehand, who are to go on missions; but it sometimes happens that an announcement, for instance, of an Elder being ordered to India, falls like a thunderbolt upon some unsuspecting saint. The English mission is one sought after by influential men, being regarded as a profitable one, pecuniarily; while the more undesirable ones are shunned, and regarded as punishments. A few years ago, Mr. Jennings, the prince of Mormon merchants, was given one of these "punishments." Of course it would have been a great sacrifice for him to have left his business, so the matter was compromised with the president, and Mr. Jennings allowed to procure a substitute. I do not know the pecuniary consideration received either by the president or the substitute. The presidency of the English mission is supported out of the tithing paid in that country; but those who are sent out to preach receive no remuneration from the church, and are supposed to fall back upon the old apostolic plan, and go forth without purse or scrip. Going without purse or scrip practically refers only to the purse of the church. Missionaries are allowed to use their own funds to any extent they desire; but to do so is unnecessary. When one is about to start the people of his ward, or settlement, ascertain his wants, and supply them in kind. That is if his wardrobe is scant, it is replenished; if his shoes are poor, others are furnished; and his larder is supplied for a journey to the next locality, where it wil be renewed. The more liberal of the Saints also furnish to the more popular of their missionaries ready cash; but this is unusual. Cash itself is exceedingly uncommon among the people.

In England, when an Elder arrives on a mission he is dealt with most liberally. The first act of the resident Mormon is to take him to a clothier, and substitute a suit of ministerial black for the variegated homespun in which he is clad. The outer man is quite renewed, and a missionary two days after his arrival in Liverpool, would not be recognized as the same individual who had landed a few days before. Their houses are then thrown open, and he fares very much as did Methodist preachers when taken into a family during the session of a conference twenty years ago; the fatted calf is killed, and everything possible done to increase the creature comforts. If he should be a polygamist, he is even more enthusiastically received, and more sumptuously entertained, being regarded by the vulgar as belonging to a higher order of beings than monogamic brothers. How different from the public feeling toward such in 1850 when Parley Pratt had to lie to the people to satisfy them! In

England, however, the Mormons know nothing more about the practical workings of polygamy than do the nuns in France.

Latterly the president of the English session has been allowed to take *one* wife with him; but this was not permitted until recently. The former prohibition resulted in conduct disgraceful to some who were sent as well as to the church that sent them. I must mention a rather romantic incident connected with the life of a president who flourished in Liverpool not a hundred years ago. While he had two wives in Salt Lake City, he became attracted by a young lady in the city where he was residing, and the intimacy resulted in their marriage. How he evaded the law of the church which requires that plural marriages shall take place only before Brigham Young I do not know; but he was married nevertheless. He may have been married over again when he returned to Zion, and perhaps reproved for having kept a mistress, for such she must have been considered by the church if he was not married according to its laws. Not long after the celebration of the nuptials, wife number one or number two turned up in Liverpool, when the president found himself in a strait, with two wives, where he would certainly be punished if it were known to the authorities. The young lady was publicly introduced as his wife, while the American wife was not known to be one. And as the husband had followed the example of Abraham in not remaining true to the wife of his youth, so he followed his example farther, and when in difficulty represented that his Sarah was his *sister*. In this the man was accidentally consistent. But as he holds up Abraham as an example, being a polygamist, he should also hold him up as an example being a prevaricator, and if his course justified the one practice, it should also the other, then polygamy and lying ought to be taught together. The president lived several months with his two wives, his first continuing to pass as his sister.

The presidents generally are held in high esteem by the resident Mormons, but such is not always the case, as may be seen from the following extract of a letter before me.

It would not be proper for me to give the name of the writer; but I would state that the person had observed all that is referred to in the letter. After alluding to other matters it refers to a certain president, whose name is given, in this wise:

"This man was a tyrant among the people, and few respected him. He would not show himself to preach to the people except on fast days once a month; and then he would scold them and tell them that they were extravagant; that they lived too well; that they did not pay enough to the Lord; and during one month seventeen old members, who had been in the church ever since its organization in Europe, were 'cut off'" (women would never have been dealt with thus harshly—they are too valuable in the church and the unfortunates must have been men). The reason people did not like him was because he spent so much money on his "little *doll*," (the wife he had with him. Saints in Salt Lake do not have "dolls"—their wives as a rule are treated as anything else). "He made it a practice to go to the theatre and take his wife's family, and that cost him one pound every night he went, and *it was the tithing that paid it*. He was just the man to extort money from the poor, and 'cut them off' if they did not pay their tithing; and a man or woman rather than lose their position in the church would pay their last cent.

"I know of cases where women have had to take their husbands' clothes to the pawnbrokers, in order to have the money ready for their teacher. Shoes have been taken from little children's feet to pay the fee. It is a common thing for a poor sister to go out and earn a shilling, and when she goes home find an Elder from Utah at her house, and she will very cheerfully put her hard-earned shilling in his hand, and believe that the Lord has blessed her for it, *and I have known cases* where the men have gone into a liquor-store and spent it." Such testimony is rather damaging to the character of Mormons when they go abroad.

Formerly the headquarters of Mormonism was in Liverpool, but within a few years they have been changed to London, and there the Elders report on their arrival out, and are sent thence to different parts of the kingdom. The manufacturing towns, where there are large numbers of operatives, and other localities where the ignorant and poor are collected, are their principal fields of operations. Their meetings are held in public halls, hired for the purpose, and large numbers are attracted by curiosity, and the more credulous among them are easily deceived by the sophistry and misrepresentations of the preachers, and unite with the church. Sometimes their meetings are held out doors, in market-places, and elsewhere, but such gatherings are often dispersed by the police. Another means of reaching the people is by meetings in the houses of those who have embraced the faith, and are zealous to extend the new gospel among their friends; accordingly they are collected together, and the teacher invited to preach. No insignificant proportion of Mormon converts have been made in this way.

A more successful way of proselyting than by preaching the ridiculous tenets of their theology, is in the extravagant praise of the Mormon's Zion, in the Great Salt Lake valley. The temporal advantages to be derived from a residence there are represented to be incalculable; and then to be comparatively shut in with God's people, away from the unbelieving and wicked Gentiles, is another desirable consideration. Some of the Elders teach that a home will spring up as if by magic, and that the fields will yield their fruit almost without cultivation. Others whose assurance is not so great, dwell more upon the spiritual benefits of a residence in Zion, but all are agreed in overrating the natural advantages of the locality. It is portrayed as equal in all respects to the Canaan which the Jews so long sought while journeying in the wilderness.

In addition to these tangible advantages, held out to a poor, ignorant, and often oppressed people, is the wonderful influence exerted by the impression created of a real interest in their spiritual welfare on the part of the missionary. They never before realized that a minister's concern for them individually, extended further than to see that they attended service occasionally, and paid regularly their church fees. They regard it as Christ-like for a man to subject himself to so many trials, without pay, and without honor, for their soul's benefit, and while they see nothing attractive in his religion, they see so much to admire in the man that they are willing to accept his teachings, and become the subjects of the salvation he preaches to them. Occasionally educated persons, who have been unfortunate in life, see in such conduct such a contrast with the characters of those surrounding them, that they too are led into the delusion.

As soon as the assent of an individual is obtained to the doctrinal teachings of an Elder, he then endeavors to impress upon the mind of the convert the importance of aiding in building up God's physical kingdom on earth, and as the advantages represented as belonging to that kingdom have probably led the individual to embrace Mormonism, he is only too willing to contribute his part by becoming at the earliest possible day a resident of Zion. But to migrate thither costs money, and those most anxous to go are least capable of meeting the expenses of the journey. For the church to pay these expenses would require a large outlay, and it provides a way for people to pay for themselves; so when their Christian privileges are preached to them, their Christian duty to enable them to enjoy these privileges is as strongly urged. This consists in raising the necessary emigration money. Nine pounds is the amount charged for the entire journey, and any portion of this, from a penny a week upward, may be deposited at the Emigration Office, until the required amount is raised. The individual is then sent over in the next emigrant vessel the church charters, after the sum has been deposited. The enthusiastic young convert will deny himself or herself (oftener herself) the ordinary comforts of life, to be able to pay their emigration fees.

There is, however, an emigration fund, raised by contribution, for the benefit of those unable to save the required amount. This is expended at the discretion of the president of the mission. He says who shall, and who shall not have the benefit of the fund. Young girls may without difficulty secure their passage without prepayment; but an educated man, with a family, may be unable to procure any of the benefits of the emigration fund if his services are useful in England. Nor indeed are such always allowed to go, when they can raise the funds, but are told they must be further "tried" before going up to Zion.

The separation of families for shipment to this country is one of the great evils of the emigration system. As an example I would mention an instance when Apostle Cannon was in charge of the mission, only three or four years ago. He allowed *fourteen young girls*, from twelve to fifteen years of age, to be taken from their parents and friends, and without a protector to embark on an emigrant vessel, and then journey almost across the continent to Salt Lake valley. Not long after their arrival a lady met one of these girls she knew in England, and inquired where her mother lived, supposing, of course, she was in the territory, and was quite surprised to learn of the circumstance I have mentioned. This girl then described the journey and remarked that soon after sailing she sprained her ankle, when she "felt the need of mother, but oh!" said she, "how much more did I need her when crossing the plains," and then related the shameful insults to which she had been subjected which the modesty of the lady would not allow her to repeat to me. What eternal disgrace should cling to the character of the man who would willingly risk and expose the virtue of helpless girls in this way!

To populate Utah with women as fast as possible, is one great end of emigration, and it is now "counselled" that poor men who are unable to raise the price for the emigration of their whole families, should send their wives and daughters first, and go afterward themselves, when they could collect sufficient means. This is reversing the order of things formerly practiced, when the husband and father went first to provide a home.

In former years the emigrants all collected at Liverpool, even from other parts of Europe; but now the ships receive their loads from ports most convenient to the localities where the emigrants reside.

The vessels chartered are the ordinary sailing emigrant ships, and the saints are provided precisely the same accommodations that sinners find when sailing in these vessels independent of Mormon Emigration Societies. Before sailing the passengers are furnished with simple rations for the voyage, and they then arrange themselves into messes, and each mess makes such provision for the voyage as their means and inclinations will permit.

The president of the mission appoints a president of the ship, and two counsellors. This organization, it may have been noticed, runs through their system. The ship's president acts in much the same capacity that a colonel would with his regiment embarked. A clerk is also appointed, who is expected to note all that transpires on the voyage, recording carefully marriages, births, deaths, etc., and incidents of interest.

A singular entry appeared in the journal of a clerk of one of the ships that came over in 1863. It was that the president had been drunk for three consecutive days and confined for that time in the hold of the vessel. To prevent a repetition of the occurrence the "counsellors" deposed him from office, that he could not have access to the brandy that was sent out for the sick, and get drunk again. Upon the arrival in Salt Lake the facts were reported to President Young and the offender was suspended from the communion of the saints; but not long thereafter Brigham relented, and reinstated the man, remarking—"Oh! he was only drunk—that was all."

On shipboard they resort to various amusements. There are regular evenings for dancing, and singing is almost constantly heard in some part of the ship. The men smoke and swear. Some of the most profane men I ever heard were Mormons. The sisters often manifest a propensity to petty larceny in the way of appropriating the stockings, and other little articles of the wardrobe of those lying next to them, after turning in for the night. Religious services are held night and morning, and at the same time the roll is called to ascertain whether or not all are safe.

A voyage of four or six weeks, under favorable circumstances, lands them in New York City, when the saints find accommodations, like other immigrants, in Castle Garden, until arrangements are completed for their transportation by rail to the Missouri River. About three days are required for this.

At one time immigrants were landed at New Orleans, and went thence up the Mississippi and Missouri Rivers to some point where their trains met them for their overland journey. This route, however, has been abandoned entirely, as an unhealthy and expensive one, and not so expeditious.

From New York the immigrants are hurried through the States in cars provided for that class of travellers, without any opportunities of observing the country or the people, and soon reach a point near Omaha, whence they commence their trip over the plains. Often they arrive in advance of the trains, which are liable to delays occasioned by the high water in streams at the season they start, and the exposed people suffer much from sickness.

From their debarkation at New York, to their arrival in Salt Lake City, they are without medical attendance, and the sick die, or recover, as the unaided powers of nature may decide the case. The hardships to which they are subjected, combined with a want of cleanliness, loss of rest, improper diet, exposure, &c., often thwart the recuperative powers of nature, and many a Mormon lies buried on the plains, who with a little care and attention, might have been saved. The employment of a doctor, under any circumstances, is regarded as an evidence of weakness of faith. The power of healing is supposed to be in the laying on of hands, which is the only means used. The large mortality in a healthy country, is evidence against their system as well as the conclusions of Oliver Wendell Holmes, who wrote that if all the medicine in the world were thrown into the sea it would be a good deal better for mankind and a good deal worse for the fishes.

Every spring the owners of wagons and teams among the Mormons of Utah are required to furnish, according to their ability, the means of transportation necessary for the immigrants. Each individual who furnishes any, keeps an account of the number of wagons or animals furnished, and if they are not returned in the fall, the owner is remunerated from the Emigration Fund; but he is allowed nothing for the use of them. He is supposed to be loaning them to the Lord, and expects to receive tenfold, in some other way, what their use may be worth. The drivers of these teams are selected with great care, and before they are sent out are required to go through the endowment house, a secret institution of Mormonism, where by oaths, and ceremonies, the initiated are supposed to be made purer, and with drivers fresh from this solemn and holy (?) service the women are supposed to be safer. Upon the arrival of the trains at the river all is life and activity among the immigrants in preparing for their long journey, and no little amusement is afforded by the sight of ox-teams, which is quite a novel thing to them.

These wagons are only for the transportation of baggage and rations. The people are all required to walk the thousand mile journey without even suitable conveyance for those who are sick on the road—such can be accommodated only on the loaded wagons. They have no tents, nor any protection from the storm. It is a sad sight to see the road lined with these people laboring to get along in a severe snow-storm, as I have seen them. Old and decrepid men and women, some with their wooden shoes, others without any, totter along in the rear of the slow-moving ox-trains; but slow as they move it is too fast for some of these who are borne down by the infirmities of age or disease. I have been informed that many such die on the road, and from what I have witnessed I cannot doubt the truth of the statement. Out of a party of nine hundred that crossed the plains in the summer of 1864, twenty-two died after leaving the Missouri River. One of this number was an old man who for some offence was ducked in a stream until he was drowned. This I learn from the lips of a witness of the murder. Another of the casualties was the destruction of a poor woman by wild beasts. From sickness and fatigue she was unable to keep up with the train, and was killed and devoured by wolves or other wild animals.

Notwithstanding all their hardships and privations, murmuring is not heard because it is not allowed. If a saint is reported for that offence, at the next meeting he is surely reprimanded for the first offence, and if he persists more severe punishment is inflicted. To counteract any tendency to complaint, and drive away the melancholy natural under such circumstances, frequent dances are indulged in, as well as other hilarity, to drown thought. Then in addition they are urged to a contented and hopeful state of mind, by frequent allusions, at their religious services, to that beautiful land flowing with milk and honey, which they are going up to possess.

Great as are their hardships in crossing the plains at present, a system was tried several years ago that deserves no milder designation than one of barbarous cruelty. I refer to the hand-cart trains. Hand-carts were substituted for wagons, and two individuals, usually a man and woman, drew each, and this cart contained all their worldly goods. If from fatigue or accident they abandoned it, they abandoned every thing. A lady at Fort Bridger, who witnessed the passage of one of these trains through that post, informed me that it was one of the most sickening sights she ever beheld. Men and women had lashed themselves with cords to their carts like beasts, and without shoes their mangled and bleeding feet trod the rough ground, as they toiled over it with their load. One of the men was wheeling his wife, who had become exhausted from fatigue, in addition to his usual load.

A friend who had opportunities of knowing whereof he wrote, thus refers to this hand-cart train: "He (referring to an apostle returning from a mission) came across the plains in a carriage, with three wagons loaded, and in one of them a piano, besides every thing needed for his journey. He passed the hand-cart train, and those who had furnished him the money, while in England, to buy what he was taking along, cried out to him to assist them; but he was *too big* to stop to hear their distress. This train, which started late in the season, was overtaken by heavy snow-storms, in November and December, and many died before they reached the valley. Brigham openly cursed the man responsible for this suffering, and he could not hold up his head for a long time. The *people's* curse still remains on him."

In addition to those who lost their lives, there are now invalids in Salt Lake City who date back their shattered health to this unfortunate experiment.

When the trains reach "Emigration Cañon" the pass through the Wasach Mountains by which they reach the city, or at some other point convenient to the city, the agents of the Emigration Society visit the people to settle the accounts of those who have not paid their emigration fees in advance. The notes of such delinquents are then taken, and these are held *in terrorem* over them if at any time they think of leaving the territory. The society expects to be reimbursed for all its expenditures for emigration.

This being settled they then proceed to the city and encamp or bivouac in Emigration Square. Upon the arrival of the trains the inhabitants visit the square to find friends, servants or wives, as they may desire. Heber Kimball advises those in charge of the trains not to select all the pretty girls before they get in, but give all a chance. Very often, when the market for wives is dull, fine-looking girls are hired as servants. Not having been such at their homes they may object at first, but after being "counselled" to go they generally yield. Probably in a short time the employer takes a fancy to the maiden and tells her that he has discovered that he "kinder likes her," and is willing to exalt her to a wife in this world and glory in the next. This proposition may be as distasteful as the first was, and she is again "counselled" and again yields. Such is common experience of immigrants.

After the party has been well culled over, and those who can do so have obtained places, the remainder are sent off to the settlements to be treated in like manner. It is a common thing for large families to be divided up to go to almost as many different localities as there are individuals, and this done without the consent of the parties. It is true they are not forcibly separated, but are "counselled" to go. This is as bad a feature as was one of the worst of negro slavery in the South a few years ago.

CHAPTER XIX.

MORMON WORSHIP AND MORMON DIGNITARIES

THE public worship of the Mormons consists of services at the Tabernacle every Sunday morning and afternoon, and also on the first Thursday of every month, which is observed as a fast day. They have meetings in the school-houses of the various wards on Sunday nights, also. Their form of public worship is similar to the services in Methodist churches on such occasions. A hymn is announced and sung, followed by a prayer, and then the discourses, after which another hymn is sung, and the congregation dismissed with a prayer, or the benediction. During the summer months, as I have before stated, services are held in the "Bowery" instead of the present Tabernacle, which is too small for the large congregations that assemble.

At both morning and afternoon service at least two sermons are preached, and the Prophet is usually one of the speakers in the afternoon, when there are the largest congregations. I have attended several meetings in the Bowery, and on the first day heard Mr. Geo. Q. Cannon, one of the Apostles, and Private Secretary to the President, address the people. The burden of his sermon (for I suppose it is styled such) was faithfulness to the church, without specifying in what it consisted, and an abuse of the Government, to which he referred rather ingeniously as "our enemies," though at times was not at all ambiguous, and spoke of "conspirators against the church by men in high places, from the head of the nation down." He declared that nowithstanding all this the church would succeed, and remarked that God had wrought greater miracles in delivering the Latter Day Saints from their enemies than he ever did in the deliverance of the children of Israel.

Though an educated man himself, he spoke very disparagingly of education in general, and alluded to the many apostacies from the faith that had occurred with young men aspiring to professions. He warned the young ladies, especially, against cultivating any taste for the fine arts. This was probably suggested by the apostacy of Miss Carmichael, a young lady of liberal education, who has written and published some very good poetry.

Mr. Cannon is an educated man, with pleasing and refined manners, and appears to have a well-balanced mind. I am not willing, therefore, to accord to him that honesty which characterizes the great mass of the people, to which I shall refer hereafter.

I have also heard the Prophet in the Tabernacle. His "say" consisted in comments upon the remarks, and a history of the religious life of a speaker who had preceded him; in the hackneyed subject of faithfulness to the church, and in abuse of the Government because of what he declared was persecution and inconsistency, and as regards the latter, branched off on political topics a little, and referred to the inconsistency of Congress, which four years ago couldn't conceive of authority enough to give the President, but now wants to take from him that delegated in the Constitution. Among other strange remarks he made was that the Latter Day Saints were the only sane people on the subject of religion on the face of the earth.

I heard the remarks of the brother to whom the President alluded. It was his first sermon in the Mormon Church, and the only one I ever heard in which there was any spirituality. His history, as I gathered from the remarks of both himself and the President, is as follows: He was educated for the ministry in Germany, and filled a pulpit in a Lutheran church in that country for a few years, when he emigrated to the United States. He found in this country no sect exactly corresponding with the Church to which he belonged at home, and selecting the one that approached nearest to it, he united himself with the Protestant Episcopal Church. Not long afterward he was given a parish somewhere in New York, and ministered unto his people for a few years, feeling, however, all this time, that he was not doing all he could for the Master. To be taught his proper and his whole duty he made a subject of special prayer, and sought in every possible way to ascertain what it was. Finally he had a vision (visions are very common with Mormons), and in it an angel came to him, and he inquired of the angel what he should do, when he was told "Go thy way." Rather vague instruction for one in ignorance of his duty, and he pressed the angel for an explanation. Then the light came. The angel said, "Go to my servant, Brigham Young, in Great Salt Lake City, and he will teach thee the way." His line of duty was then clear to him; he gave up his church; corresponded with the Prophet; afterward removed to Utah, and is now an honest Mormon.

The following day I had an interview with the Prophet, and mentioned that I heard him preach the day before, when he inquired if I heard the sermon preceding his, and appeared to be very proud of this new accession to his clergy. He said the man had been a student all his life, and had never done a day's manual labor before he arrived in Utah; "but when he came here we put him to work as we do everybody."

It grieved me to see a pious and educated man led into this ridiculous delusion.

The fact of this man being educated was not a source of congratulation to Brigham, but his complete infatuation and submission were the great things. An idea of the President's appreciation of education may be learned from the following:

On Sunday afternoon, in the Bowery of Salt Lake, before 3000 persons, during the summer of 1855, Orson Pratt was addressing the people on the necessity of studying from books. Said he:

"Suppose you and I were deprived of all books, and that we had faith to get revelation, and no disposition to understand that which has been sought out, understood and recorded in books, what would be our condition? It would require an indefinite period in which to make any progress in the knowledge that is even now extant."

Brigham rose, his dignity hurt, his temper ruffled, and he administered to Pratt, the presumptuous offender, one of the most outrageous tongue-lashings ever conceived of. He said:

"The professor has told you that there are many books in the world, and I tell you there are many people in the world; he says there is something in all these books, I say each one of these persons has a name; he says it would do you good to learn that something, and I say it would do you just as much good to learn these somebodies' names. Were I to live to the age of Methuselah, and every hour of my life learn something new out of some of these books, and remember every particle I had acquired, five minutes' revelation would teach me more truth, and more right, than all this nonsense that I should have packed in my unlucky brains."

The sacrament of the Lord's Supper is administered every Sunday afternoon. Water is substituted for wine (which was formerly used, but has been abandoned because too expensive) as one of the emblems, and after being blessed is passed around through the congregation, during the delivery of the sermon, and appeared to me as any other than a solemn service. The water and bread is blessed by Bishop Hunter, the Chief Bishop, and passed by three Elders selected for that office, to the President, his two colleagues, and then to the others on the stand in the order of rank. Teachers and priests, a lower class of officials, then distribute the emblems through the congregation.

Fasting on Sunday morning before going to "meeting" is enjoined upon all the members, and they are expected to contribute the value of the breakfast thus saved to charitable purposes.

The exercises in the Bowery I would not have supposed to be of a religious character if the hymns and prayers had been omitted; and those of the ward-meetings partake much less of worship, though they are called religious meetings. They are presided over by the Bishops, who explain to the people the most successful ways of raising poultry, cattle, etc., and settle any little disputes that may have occurred during the week about their irrigating, water, etc. Should a sister have been seen taking butter or eggs or any article to Camp Douglas, to realize a little cash from their sale, her Bishop is very likely at the next ward-meeting, to give the sisters a lecture about being too intimate with Gentiles, and to refer very plainly to the conduct of the offending one.

The grand religious occasions of the year are during the sessions of the semiannual conferences in April and October. These meetings are for the transaction of church business, by the Bishops and others, when their presence in a collective capacity is necessary, but the laity are also assembled to elect officers and attend religious services. During the sessions, which continue for four or five days, there is service morning and afternoon of each day at the Bowery, but the extensive accommodations it affords are very inadequate for the occasions. The people collect in vast crowds, and stand patiently within sight, but not within hearing of the speaker, reminding me of the scene at an inauguration of a President in Washington, when a large proportion of the crowd are unable to hear a word that is said, but appear very much interested in the gesticulations of the speaker. Conference days the city is crowded with people. Every variety of vehicle to be observed at a country camp-meeting may be seen standing about the streets, and the enthusiasm of the people is kept up by bands of music playing near Temple Square on Main street. They are great days in Zion !

Frequent efforts have been made by the Mormons to conduct Sabbath-schools in Salt Lake City, but so far they have all proved failures, generally not continuing for more than three days.

Recently a Gentile Sabbath-school has been started and promises to be very successful. At one time a number of Mormon children attended, but the edict of the President, forbidding them to do so, went forth, and they were withdrawn.

The Mormons are exceedingly fond of dancing, which is regarded as a very important part of their education.

During the winter there are dances two or three times a week in every ward, and on special occasions, such as religious and other anniversaries, grander entertainments are given by the prominent in the church in "Social Hall," a building owned by Brigham, and rented for such purposes.

From these social gatherings the Gentiles are not excluded, the more liberal of them being usually invited. A better state of feeling exists between the officers stationed at Camp Douglas and the Mormon authorities, than during the incumbency of General Connor as Commandant of that post. These officers and their families are occasionally invited, and attend these entertainments, without in the least compromising themselves. General Connor would have regarded such conduct a sufficient cause for dismissal.

Like the Irishman who thought "St. Patrick a greater man than the Fourth of July," the Mormons regard the 26th of July, the day on which they reached the valley, as altogether a more important anniversary than our Independence Day. It is celebrated by reviews of the militia, parades, picnics, social convivial parties, special theatrical performances, etc. The more extensive of these demonstrations take place biannually. Last year it was celebrated only by an extra performance at the theatre, and a partial suspension of business. Those whose loyalty to

Mormonism led them to close their stores were honored by a band of music playing in front of each closed store about noon. The Fourth of July is but little regarded by the saints.

There is nothing peculiar in the dress of the Mormons. It presents a great variety of styles, unequalled in that respect by any people. The wives and daughters of the President generally dress tastefully and fashionably, as do many other ladies in Salt Lake City. The masses of the people wear every variety and style of garment worn in any part of Europe during the last century, but the majority wear cloth of their own making. I was much amused one day, during their last semiannual conference, at the appearance of a sister who came into the Bowery shortly after I had been seated there. She was probably one of the late arrivals. Her dress attracted the attention of even her sisters, who have become accustomed to every variety. The striking peculiarity was a white lace veil of immense size, most elaborately embroidered, which was thrown over a decidedly antique-looking bonnet, and hanging to the waist all around. It reminded me of one my mother had when I was a boy, something less than fifty years ago, that she preserved as a curiosity of the times when her grandmother was a girl. The dress of the men is about as varied as that of the women. I have frequently seen the clergy go into the pulpit with linen coats and no vests; and on one very hot day I think I saw a brother, who was actively engaged in passing the bread and water from the stand to those who administered it to the congregation, in his shirt-sleeves.

I should have remarked before that education is most shamefully neglected. They have no system of public schools. There are schools in each ward, and during the months of November, December, and January, are pretty well attended by scholars of both sexes, varying from five to twenty-five years of age, but the standard of education in them is very low. During the winter months a school will number seventy-five scholars; but as soon as the farming season begins, it will fall off to fifteen or twenty, and those that remain are very young—little children of six or eight years, who are sent from home to be kept out of mischief. The teachers of these schools are not paid by the city, but the parents are charged for the children they send. The fees received are usually vegetables, fruit, butter, &c. The schools of Salt Lake City are quite in keeping with Brigham's ideas of education referred to elsewhere.

I will now endeavor to give an account of the appearance, &c., of the Prophet and his prominent associates.

A few days after my arrival at Camp Douglas, I gratified my curiosity by calling upon the President at his residence. I was received in his private office, and no one being present but his second colleague and the gentleman who introduced me, I had a good opportunity of conversing with the remarkable man, and of observing him under favorable circumstances.

As I stated to the gentleman who accompanied me, that I was actuated only by curiosity in desiring to see his friend who had become so noted a character, and with this knowledge he invited me to go, so I feel more at liberty to make public my impressions of him gathered from that interview than I would under different circumstances. Moreover, Brigham Young is a public character, and all such must expect to be criticised. Mr. Young is a native of Vermont, was born in 1801, and is remarkably well preserved for a man of his age. I should not have recognized him as the individual I had seen in the "Bowery," or the one whose photograph I had obtained. He appeared not so large, nor was his bearing as commanding or dignified. His forehead is contracted and his eyes small, with cunning well depicted in them, and giving him a reserved expression. His mouth of moderate size, with thin compressed lips, and a prominent chin, indicating decision. His hair is sandy, mixed with silvery threads, and his unshaven face, with beard of two weeks' growth, which he was making into whiskers, gave to it the usual unsightly appearance under such circumstances. At first he seemed inclined to reticence, but in a few minutes this passed off, and he conversed freely and even perpetrated a joke. Whenever I spoke he seemed to observe my countenance closely, as if studying my character in my physiognomy. His health is robust and his habits exceedingly regular. He never employs a doctor for himself or any member of his family. He is said to be the best dancer in Salt Lake City, and, though sixty-six years of age, trips across the floor as lightly and with all the fancy steps of a young dancing-master. He is fond of the amusement, and indulges freely in it at social parties. He is also an admirer of the drama, and is seldom absent from the theatre when there is a performance; has a box used only by himself and last wife, and occasionally some friend or relative. These latter habits are hardly in keeping with his position as prophet, seer, revelator and translator of the Church of Latter Day Saints.

I was rather disappointed in the man. I think he is without that strength of intellect which is generally attributed to him by both Mormon and Gentile. He is unquestionably a man of indomitable will, of great diplomacy, of remarkable business capacity, and, as a financier, is probably without an equal west of the Missouri River; and as a leader of a fanatical religious people under the most trying circumstances, history furnishes none who have surpassed him. His early advantages of education have not been great, nor has he improved himself very much in riper years. His pronunciation is decidedly bad, and his bad grammar cannot be altogether the result of carelessness. His general information I should think was very good. I was treated with much courtesy, and after he had laid aside his reserve, which any man so much an object of curiosity would be expected to acquire, to a greater or less extent, his social qualities met my admiration. I persisted in addressing him as Mr. Young, rather to the annoyance of my friend, who always styled him Mr. President in conversation. Upon rising to leave we shook hands, and walking toward the door he cordially invited me to call again.

I had no conversation with the Second President, Heber C. Kimball, to whom I referred as being present, but when

about leaving he shook me warmly by the hand and asked that the blessing of the Lord might follow me. He is about the age of Brigham Young, is a large muscular man, and neither his appearance or conversation would lead a stranger to suspect that he was the second president of a religious sect. He was a blacksmith before he joined the Mormons, and looks not unlike one now. He has a Sun-of-Thunder style of delivering his harangues from the pulpit. His elocution would cause Professor Bailey of Yale to faint, and his irreverence would be pronounced profanity by any Christian minister I know, except, perhaps, one I once met in Washington, who is somewhat of the same manner of man. But irreverence is not the striking peculiarity of his sermons They often partake of such disgusting obscenity that a sense of propriety and modesty will not allow me to refer to here even in general terms. And still he publicly declares that his sermons are not prepared beforehand, but he speaks only *as he is moved by the Holy Spirit.* One might suppose the influence of some other spirit operated. The editor of the *Millennial Star* was once severely reproved for modifying the sermons of Mr. Kimball, so that they would not shock the English reader with their vulgarity and indecency. He was sternly directed to publish them literally as he received them. Mr. Kimball acknowledges the most profound allegiance to "Brother Brigham," and pays to him all the homage of the most humble of the Mormons. He is wealthy, and is reported as having a greater number of wives than Brigham Young—how many I am unable to say. He is illiterate and vulgar in every sense of the word. Knowing the man by reputation, I did not feel safer or more comfortable after receiving his benediction.

Mr. Daniel H. Wells, the Third President, is a man of considerably over fifty years, tall, spare, with a thin, sharp face, and a prominent crooked nose, presenting altogether a very ungainly appearance for a Mormon President or Lieutenant-General. In the latter capacity he was in the field in command of the army of saints in 1857-8, when they occupied a position in Echo Cañon, to which I have referred in a previous chapter. I have not been in the society of Mr. Wells, but learn that he is quite illiterate, and is an honest Mormon.

He is a much more moderate polygamist than either of his colleagues—having *only* seven wives. They were all taken from the humblest walks of life.

But few of the other leaders of the church are known to fame, and I will not occupy space in referring to them, as I have the three presidents. Orson Hyde, John Taylor, George Q. Cannon and Orson Pratt, are probably the best educated men among them. The last-named is regarded as the philosopher of the church. I quoted him in my last in explaining doctrinal points. He is regarded with a good deal of jealousy by the President, who in consequence keeps him most of the time on missions, or other duty requiring him to be absent from Zion.

Orson Hyde is also regarded as a dangerous man. He is a brilliant orator, and a good writer. His associates, who are fearful and jealous on account of his abilities, and his presumption sometimes in preaching in a way not very satisfactory to the President, style him the "*big head.*" He is said to have apostatized during the life of Smith, the first Prophet, and afterward joined the church again.

The large majority of their preachers are exceedingly illiterate, and it is torturing to sit and hear their bad English, when there is an entire absence of argument or point in their remarks.

The masses should receive more notice than I can give them in this article. Nine-tenths, if not nineteen-twentieths, as I have before stated, are converts to the faith through the labors of missionaries in England, Wales, Scotland and Denmark. There are but few Germans among them, fewer Irish, and still fewer Americans, though the principal officers are natives of this country, and Brigham manages always to keep it so.

I must add a few words about the people as they are found here. After settling in Utah, whatever may have been their previous pursuits, the people with great unanimity turn their attention to agricultural pursuits, and raising of cattle. It constitutes them a more independent people, and indeed such is necessary, as there is but little market for manufactured articles. They live upon the products of their farms, or what they use that is not produced there, some article that is, is traded for it. I imagine that there are many Mormons who have been several years in Utah who have never seen a greenback or piece of coin during their residence there.

Notwithstanding their industry and thriftiness, they remain poor, because of the little sale there is for their produce, and the tax of the church upon every thing. One-tenth of all the profits of the merchant, of the pay of the laborer, and of the products of the farmer, go directly into the tithing office. This rule is universal, and knows no exception.

Of the honesty and uprightness in business transactions and general good moral character of the *masses*, particularly in the smaller settlements, I can speak as complimentary as I can of their industry and frugality.

Some of my lady readers would be pleased, I have no doubt, to read a description of the more prominent of their sex; but I am unable to give that from personal observation, or association with them. When I called upon the President his courtesy and hospitality did not extend to an invitation to visit a few of the Mrs. Youngs or his daughters. I will, however, give a description of Amelia, the last wife of Brigham, as drawn by Mrs. Wait. Before doing so I would with all deference to the author suggest that it be received *cum grano salis*. It is not only extravagant, but parts of it inconsistent with her own delineations of the character of Brigham given elsewhere in the same book. She says:

"Amelia Folsom is a native of Portsmouth, New Hampshire. She is tall, well formed, with light hair and gray eyes, and regular features. She is quite pale, owing to ill health. Has but little refinement of manner. When at the theatre sitting in the king's box with her husband, the observed of all observers, she may be seen eating apples, throwing the skins about, chatting with Brigham, and occasionally levelling her glass at some one in the assembly. She plays and sings with indifferent skill and taste. She was for a long time unwilling to marry the President, but he continued his suit with a pertinacity worthy of a better cause; and by repeated promises of advancement made to herself and her parents, finally succeeded. For several months he urged his suit, during which time his carriage might be seen almost any day standing at her father's door, for hours at a time. He told her she was created expressly for himself, and could marry no one else, on pain of everlasting destruction. She plead, protested, and wept, but he persevered, and at length, when all other arguments failed, he told her he had received a special revelation from heaven on the subject. She had always believed in Mormonism, and had been taught to have faith in revelation. 'Amelia,' he said, 'you must be my wife. God has revealed it to me. You cannot be saved by any one else. If you will marry me I will save you and exalt you to be a queen in the celestial world; but if you refuse you will be destroyed, both soul and body!'

"The poor girl believed in this impostor, and yielding to his wishes became his wife. For several months after her marriage Amelia was sad and dejected, but of late she has rallied, and appears the gayest of the gay.

* * * * * *

"Amelia is evidently living under constraint, and acting an assumed character. She is playing the *rôle* of a happy wife with a broken heart. At the time of her marriage her heart had been given to another to whom she should have been married. That she compromised her character in marrying Young under these circumstances, is a fact too notorious to be concealed.

"Nevertheless, Amelia stands the recognized queen of the harem. She leads the *ton* and is the envied woman of the saints. Thousands bow low as she passes, and think themselves happy to receive her passing recognition. [This is literally ridiculous and untrue; no more homage is paid to her than to any other woman.] She is now a queen, and is to be a goddess in the celestial world. The new wife is sometimes restive and impatient, and treats her liege lord shabbily. She is at times notional and imperious, and somewhat coquettish—to all of which her husband submits with good grace for the present and pets her as a child.

* * * * * *

"The theatre was dedicated by prayer and a grand ball. This was in the winter of 1862-63. Brigham led off in the dance with Amelia, and all was smiles and sunshine. On another occasion he honored another of the women with his hand for the first cotillon. This so displeased Amelia that she refused to dance with him at all. He coaxed, she shrugged her shoulders and shook her head. It was only after much solicitation on his part that she granted her forgiveness and consented to dance with him.

* * * * * *

"Amelia is tyrannical, and rules the women of the harem with a strong hand. Poor Emmeline (she next preceded Amelia as the favorite) is quite broken-hearted. Naturally very sensitive, she lives to drag out a miserable life."

In fact, all the women are unhappy and miserable. A common remark in reply to the usual salutation is, "Oh, I've got the blues to-day."

One of the noted characters among the Mormons that I have not mentioned is Porter Rockwell, said to have been the leader of the Danites, or "Avenging Angels." It is represented that this band was employed in making way with such as became obnoxious to the Mormon hierarchy. That many have disappeared mysteriously, or been "killed by the Indians" when the Indians were committing no depredations, cannot be doubted, but whether or not Porter Rockwell has the blood of such victims on his skirts I cannot say. I think it doubtful whether he is more guilty than many others. He does not look like a murderer, and it is my impression that the Danite Band has been a good deal of a bugbear. Gentiles feared the Destroying Angels as negroes in our Southern cities fear the doctors after dark. I would not have the reader infer from this that I believe the Mormons above such acts, for on that subject I have something to add in my next, but I doubt if Porter has been more guilty than others. The weight of opinion with Gentiles in Utah is against me in this particular.

Porter Rockwell has become exceedingly fond of whiskey in these latter days, and but seldom visits the city without getting drunk. On such occasions he manifests none of that violence which one might suppose would then almost certainly exhibit itself in one so desperate as he is represented to be. When drunk he is perfectly harmless, and the exuberance of vitality on such occasions is relieved by loud shouts, which may be heard for squares. He is otherwise orderly and well-behaved, even when drunk. He wears his hair long, and a friend informed me that he has not cut it since the murder of Joseph Smith, and says he will not until he has avenged his death upon the man who shot him. He may be more especially the avenging angel of Joseph the martyr, if not one in general.

CHAPTER XX.

CRIMES OF THE MORMONS AND HOW MORMONISM MAY BE ERADICATED.

THE leaders of the Mormon Church claim to be tolerant; but they are so only so far as their tolerance may conduce to their interests. That they have been guilty of rigid persecution of those whose acts seemed to endanger the success of their corrupt sect, and that they have been prompted by malice and desire for revenge in perpetrating the grossest crimes, are indisputable facts.

One of the most cowardly and bloody massacres that I have seen recorded took place on the tenth of September, 1857, at Mountain Meadows, a valley in a sparsely settled country, about three hundred miles south of Salt Lake City. The history of this horrible tragedy is briefly as follows:

In the summer of 1857, a large train, with emigrants for California, consisting of men, women and children to the number of about one hundred and forty persons, passed through Salt Lake City, and proceeded southward on the usual route to Los Angelos. When they reached the locality where the bloody tragedy I am about relating was enacted, their stock was first run off by what appeared to be *Indians*, but really *Mormons* disguised as such. Their enemies making hostile demonstrations, the emigrants got together their wagons, and throwing up earth about them made a work of defence. Their assailants occupied the hills around, and fought them for several days without gaining any advantage. Finding it impossible to capture them without serious loss, they resorted to strategy and deception. Several prominent Mormons took a wagon and went around so as to approach the emigrants from the head of the meadows, and as they did so exhibited a white flag. The emigrants recognizing white men in the wagon allowed them to approach, and held up a little girl dressed in white to answer the signal. The Mormons entered the fort. They represented that they had talked with the "Indians," and found them very furious—determined to capture the party at all hazards; but that they (the Mormons) would negotiate with the "Indians" for terms of surrender if it was desired. They were requested to do so, and after a short absence returned with the "Indians'" alternative—the surrender of *everything*, and their lives would be spared. In addition to the purported agreement on the part of the assailants, as their part of the treaty, not to injure the emigrants personally, the Mormon negotiators proposed to furnish an escort of forty armed men to conduct them back to the settlements. Harsh as were the terms, they were accepted; the presence of helpless women and children doubtless influencing the emigrants in their decision. The escort arrived, and the unsuspecting emigrants abandoned everything, and marched out of their fort. The women and children were in front, the men behind them, and the guard in the rear of all. In this order they marched a short distance, when at a given signal the "Indians" rushed upon the party, shooting dead by the first volley, the men and afterward the women and children, except seventeen of the latter who were supposed to be too young to tell the tale of this horrid butchery. No injury was sustained by the escort.

Judge Cradlebaugh very graphically describes this massacre in a speech he delivered in the House of Representatives, when a delegate from Nevada Territory. The Judge appends to the speech the affidavits of a number of individuals, that convict, beyond all question, the Mormons as the perpetrators of this crime. The evidence of their guilt may be summed up as follows: First, the statements of friendly Indians, giving the particulars so minutely, and so in accordance with known facts, as to be of themselves very strong evidence. They explained how the Mormons disguised themselves, and pointed out the place where they assumed the disguise. Second, the testimony of apostate Mormons, who resided in the locality, and knew of the plans of the murderers, and how they were executed. Third, the testimony of some who actually participated in the crime, and afterward went to Judge Cradlebaugh at night, being afraid to do so by daylight, and gave a full account of the horrible affair. These parties offered to go before a court of justice, and testify to the facts if they could be guaranteed protection in their lives after doing so. The statements of these parties corroborated the statements of the Indians. Fourth, the statement of the children who escaped, who were old enough to observe and remember. In speaking of these children the Judge remarked: "I recollect one of them, John Calvin Sorrow, after he found he was safe, and before he was brought away from Salt Lake City, although not then nine years of age, sitting in a contemplative mood, no doubt thinking of the extermination of his family, saying, "Oh, I wish I was a man! I know what I would do. I would shoot John D. Lee; I saw him shoot my mother, and I shall never forget how he looked."

In addition to what has been stated already Major (afterward Major-General) Fitz-John Porter, Assistant Adjutant-General of Gen. A Sidney Johnston, in his official report, directly charges this crime upon the Mormons; and Mr. A. Forney, Superintendent of Indian Affairs, after a most minute and careful investigation, arrived at the conclusion that the concoctors and principal perpetrators of the massacre were Mormons, the Indians acting only a secondary part.

Brigham Young, who was at the time Superintendent of Indian Affairs in the territory, Mr. Forney not succeeding him until 1859, made no allusion to the massacre wh ch was so manifestly his duty to have done, if the Indians participated at all, in his annual report. Nor did he for a long time refer to it in the pulpit, and when he did so, of course it was to deny the guilt of the Mormons.

Any amount of presumptive evidence might be cited that points to the guilt of the Mormons; but their complicity as well as their responsibility for the Mountain Meadow massacre, is a fact too well substantiated to admit of a doubt by an impartial mind, and will ever live in history a foul stigma upon the characters of the Mormon leaders.

Some years after the horrible murder, General Carlton marched a column of troops by the locality, when he found the bones of the slain still bleaching upon the meadow. Here and there lay a skull, with the long hair attached, indicating the sex of the murdered, and interspersed with the others were the small bones of the children. Even then, an officer declares the sight to have been horrible and sickening. The General had these bones collected and buried, and over the spot he made a mound from which was raised a wooden cross, and on it he placed the inscription: "Vengeance is mine, and I will repay, saith the Lord." Not long afterward Brigham Young visited the locality, and about the same time the rude monument was demolished.

As to the perpetration of other crimes in the same locality, by the same parties, I will refer again to the speech of Judge Cradlebaugh. On this subject he remarks:

"Sitting as committing magistrate, complaint after complaint was made before me of murders, and robberies. Among these I may mention as particularly and shockingly prominent the murder of Forbes, the assassination of the Parishes and Potter, of Jones and his mother, of the Aiken party, of which there were six in all, and worst and darkest in the appalling catalogue of blood, was the cowardly and cold-blooded butchery and robbery at the Mountain Meadows."

That these crimes might be brought before the law, and the perpetrators punished, the Judge established a court in the vicinity, with military protection, and impannelled a grand jury of Mormons, of course, as there were no other residents to compose it, and their attention was called to the cases before alluded to; but "the jury thus instructed, though kept in session two weeks, utterly refused to do anything, and were finally discharged as an evidently useless appendage of a court of justice." This jury furnishes an example of the fact, to which I have elsewhere referred, that a Mormon jury would not convict a Mormon prisoner.

But Judge Cradlebaugh was determined to leave nothing undone that was in his power to do, to bring the criminals to punishment; and as the grand jury would not find a "bill," he decided to issue bench-warrants, which were placed in the hands of the marshal, aided by a military *posse*, when a general stampede took place among the Mormons; and, says the Judge, "what I want most particularly to call your attention to as a particularly noticeable fact, that this occurred more among the church officials and civil officers."

Another act of barbarity occurred in 1862. A band of disaffected Mormons (disaffected so far as the rule of Brigham was concerned) separated from the church under the leadership of one Morris, and were known as the Morrisites. He established a settlement on the Weber River. A dispute arose between the Morrisites and Brighamites, as to the authority of the latter to impose fines, and levy taxes upon a people who claimed the same right to exercise an independent government as had those who oppressed them. For some offence, the Morrisites resisted a civil officer of Brigham's government, when the official obtained a large armed posse, and again visited the settlement to serve the writs. Foolishly the Morrisites still resisted, and retaining the fanaticism they had acquired under Brigham, they were presumptuous enough to accept battle. Being very much in the minority, they were compelled to surrender, and did so, giving up their arms. The Mormon sheriff then rode into their fort, inquired for Morris, when a poor old helpless fanatic was pointed out to him, and drawing his pistol shot him dead in cold blood. Two or three of the party were murdered in the same way.

As late as last November, a most cowardly and dastardly murder was committed in Salt Lake City, under circumstances which would seem to implicate the church authorities. The murdered man was a Dr. Robinson, a Gentile, who had lived in the city for several years, and practiced his profession as a physician; and the circumstances were these: One evening, after the doctor had retired, two individuals called at his house, and requested his professional services, representing that a friend had a fractured thigh. The doctor immediately dressed, and started on what he supposed a mission of mercy, and after proceeding a few squares was shot through the head, and died shortly afterward, remaining unconscious from the time he received the wound. Mrs. Robinson knew of the two men calling, but did not know who they were. Notwithstanding the most searching investigation on the part of the Chief Justice and the Governor, no clue whatever could be had to the murderers.

The suspicious circumstances connected with Dr. Robinson's murder are these: He had been for some time conducting a suit against the Mormon authorities for the possession of the land upon which the Warm Springs are located. He claimed a preëmption right to the property, which the Mormons refused to recognize, and the church, or the city, or Brigham Young, or all combined, also claimed the ownership, and held possession of the property. Taking into consideration these facts, together with that of his being a Gentile, and a kind, gentle and popular man, without personal enemies to the knowledge of any of his friends, is well calculated to cast suspicion upon the Mormon authorities. The Gentiles who have lived longest in the city, and ought to understand the people best, are strongly of the opinion that there was complicity on the part of some of those who every Sabbath occupy seats in the pulpit at the Bowery.

On the other hand the Mormon press most violently denounce the murder, and Brigham Young, and the principal of their merchants, have become subscribers for a reward for the arrest of the murderers. This the anti-Mormons pronounce to be in keeping with the acts of saints generally, under such circumstances, and done to divert suspicion.

About the time of the Robinson murder, several other citizens of Salt Lake narrowly escaped the severe vengeance of the Mormons, for an offence which is the only one Dr. Robinson is known to have committed against them—that of claiming public lands in the vicinity of Zion. These lands have not been surveyed, nor brought into market, and the parties that settled upon them considered that they were subject to the same laws that govern other unsurveyed public land. Several small tracts of these were preëmpted and occupied. Among other settlers was Dr. Williamson, who had erected a temporary building on a quarter section near the Jordan. A raid was made on all such about the same time, and their buildings destroyed. Some of the parties came near being roughly handled, and among them the doctor, who was caught, tied, and wrapped in an old tent, preparatory to making a literal Jordan his entrance way into eternity; but he was not the least disconcerted by their conduct, and very coolly informed the mob that he would prefer that they should "shoot him as they would a dog, rather than drown him as they would a cat." Whether they admired his coolness, so as to induce them to desist, or the whole was intended as a scare, I am unable to say. The doctor being unable to take possession of lands in Zion took one of her fair daughters. I afterward saw him married to Miss Carmichael, the apostate poetess, to whom I have before alluded, and shaking off the dust of the wicked city from their feet, the bride and groom proceeded eastward to the States.

While the preëmption excitement was rife, it was frequently the theme of pulpit discourses, and one Sabbath afternoon, when a large congregation had assembled in the Bowery, Brigham alluded to this subject, and commenting upon the acts of the Gentile settlers, remarked that if one of them should go on *his land* (referring to land unlawfully granted to him by the territorial legislature) he would "Give him a preëmption to a small tract that would last him to the day of judgment"—meaning that he should have a grave. This remark, considered in connection with the assassination of Dr. Robinson, for an offence which the President declares would justify murder, leads some the more strongly to suspect that the doctor's murder was by authority.

The Mormons are an enigma to the Christian world, and the question "What holds together this strange people?" has been asked me more than once, and the same question, I have no doubt, has arisen in the minds of some who have read these chapters.

It might be answered almost as briefly as propounded, "Their own infatuation, and the ability of Brigham Young, as their leader."

With a view to enlighten the public who may feel any interest in the matter, I have referred to the different features of their history as a sect, and to their character as individuals—to their virtues, as well as to their vices—and my motives have been as little influenced by prejudice in one instance as in the other. I have received no favors to prompt words of praise; nor have I been injured to incite words of condemnation. The conclusions which I may submit, are drawn from a careful study of the people, and I would fain hope that something contained in these chapters may tend to promote the accomplishment of two great ends—the removal of a disgrace from the nation, and the enlightenment of an ignorant, deluded people.

I will endeavor to explain why I have answered the interrogatory about the unity of the Mormons as I have. Several times already I have alluded to the masses—to their deplorable ignorance, and religious enthusiasm. As a whole, a more honest and conscientious people are not to be found, nor a people so completely controlled by the will of one man. Brigham Young is worshipped as a god, and considered as incapable of error. He tells them they are the chosen people of the Almighty, and that the Mormon Church is ultimately to cover the face of the whole world. Not only earthly possessions, but celestial glory, await the faithful, and more particularly those who endure the afflictions of the church, in this her hour of trial. They are taught that the Government is the enemy of the church, as are all individuals not within her pale. The people believe it all, and nothing that the Prophet requires is considered too great a sacrifice; and nothing that the instincts of their nature, and the education of their whole lives teach them to be a crime, is regarded as other than a virtue if enjoined by him. They consider that they are doing God service in murdering helpless immigrant women and children, or becoming the assassin, in the dark hour of night, when their victim is on a mission of mercy.

That they so understand their duty is evidenced in a conversation between Mr. Colfax and his companions, and Brigham Young and his associates, on an occasion to which I have once before alluded. The subject of polygamy was being discussed and their usual arguments in its defence—the practice of the ancient church, and God's revelation to Joseph Smith—were advanced. In explanation, one of the saints contended that their understanding of God's will was above all human law, and they understood it to be His will that they should multiply wives. A hypothetical case was then submitted, and the brother asked if he should be taught that it was God's will for him to kill his son, or his enemy, would he do so. The reply was prompt in the affirmative. Then how is God's will communicated? They believe, most implicitly, through their Revelator, their President. His commands, to the Mormon, are the commands of Heaven. If Brigham Young tells a saint to murder his son, or his enemy, as a sacrifice, that saint tells us he would do so. Where is greater infatuation than this? or where more dangerous power in the hands of one man?

I can more easily understand the people than I can understand their leader, and have been in doubt whether to regard him as an impostor, or class him in the same category as his followers. The man viewed from one stand-point would appear as honest in the discharge of a stern, religious duty, and when viewed from another he would appear as an impostor. There is but little doubt of his honesty when he embraced Mormonism; and his devotion to the sect, when there was no prospect of personal benefit in life following, even in her darkest hours, when everything seemed to foreshadow its destruction, cannot be accounted for on selfish motives.

But without discussing this question further I will admit the *possibility* of his being sincere; but at the same time I must believe him to be unscrupulous as to the means he uses to accomplish his plans. His acts must be upon that corrupt principle, that the end justifies the means, and he does what he *knows* to be evil with the hope that good may result. If he is honest in his present conceptions of right and truth, such honesty must be the result of gradual education of his conscience. While I can conceive of the possibility of this, I cannot conceive of the possibility of a man of Brigham Young's opportunities being always so morally blinded. I think that, now, he may do much for expediency, that would have been very repugnant to his ideas of propriety twenty years ago.

An impostor is dangerous only so far as he may be able to carry his deception. In his practices he is controlled somewhat by reason, as to his surroundings; and is mindful of the consequences of over-reaching probabilities, as deter mined by the judgments of the class upon whom he desires to operate. He sees the prospect of failure, if he neglects to do so, and is controlled by a regard for law, which will punish him, if violated. He avoids bringing his system into collision with a stronger one, and will not defy a stronger power.

But with the fanatic it is different. His reason is impaired. He sees things from a different stand-point, and fails to realize what is extravagant in his pretensions, and his extravagancies are often the cause of his success with the weak and visionary. They see the unsoundness of his reasoning, but are captivated by his enthusiasm, and apparent honesty of purpose. He establishes a standard of his own, and is uninfluenced by the opinions of others. A fanatic on a scientific theory may become ridiculous; while a fanatic on religion may be dangerous as well as ridiculous. His honest convictions of duty may lead him to commit acts that are discountenanced by society, and punishable by law; but he is governed by his ideas of accountability to a higher law. He defies punishment, believing that any he may receive will redound to his ultimate benefit. A religious fanatic, then, is more dangerous than an impostor, and the extent to which he is dangerous is determined by his power and influence. Brigham Young I consider a more dangerous man, if honest, than he would be if an impostor. Joseph Smith, I think it has been clearly proven, was an impostor. His success was not attributable to the plausibility of his dogmas, so much as to his enthusiasm, and more than that, to the enthusiasm of the *honest* followers of a *dishonest* leader. United with their fanaticism was the cunning of Smith, which gave Mormonism its start; and then following the martyrdom of their Prophet, as they regarded him, the zeal of this credulous people increased tenfold. The unfortunate murder of this Smith, has entailed Mormonism on the country to the present day. Had he lived ten years longer, in my opinion, the sect which he founded would be only a chapter in the history of the past.

Brigham Young is unquestionably a far abler leader than

was Joseph Smith. He has proven himself a most extraordinary man. He has overcome obstacles that would have disheartened the most sanguine. He removed his people far away into a comparatively unknown country, and settled on a barren waste, which was transformed into the most fertile and productive valley in the West. He shared in their toils and privations when necessary, and afterward enriched himself on their labor when opportunity offered. He has been the greatest despot in the world, and at the same time made his subjects believe him to be their greatest benefactor!

I have spoken of the honesty and infatuation of the people, and the influence of their leader over them. Another cause operating to bind them together is their isolation, and the ignorance in which they are kept alike of the teachings of Christianity and civilization. Is it strange, therefore, that the Mormons have existed for so many years as they have?

The existence of the sect I think will terminate with the life of their able leader. This is the opinion of all observing people who have familiarized themselves with the history of the Mormons.

But it is the duty of the Government, as well as the Christian Church, to relieve the country of a sect sanctioning immorality and violating law. While the military power might be used in punishing the guilty, and compelling a greater regard for the letter of the law, it can do nothing in removing the delusions of the people; and the introduction of punishment would be immediately followed by increased fanaticism. To eradicate the evil the influences of Christianity are also required. While the Government needs the coöperation of the Church, the Church equally needs the support of the strong arm of the Government. Let the Mormons be enlightened, their judgments convinced of their error, and then protect them in their individual rights, as citizens of the United States, so as to allow them to renounce their allegiance to Mormonism and live independently of a sect that has controlled their consciences, as well as their lives, and the most favorable results will follow. An example of the practicability of such measures, may be seen in the results of the labors of an army chaplain at Camp Douglas, who exerted some influence for good among the Mormons of Salt Lake, and then they went to that post for protection. Give them protection in their own homes, and ten times the amount of good would follow the same labor.

Their infatuation is to a great extent attributable to their ignorance, and their belief in Mormonism is not oftener shaken because no access can be had to them. That conviction of their error is not impossible, is further proved by the dissensions that have occurred, notwithstanding the persecutions these incurred.

The first of these took place in 1852, through the influence of one Bishop Gladden, who became the leader of dissenters who were known as the Gladdenites. As soon as the existence of the party was known, the apostates, as they were called, were most bitterly denounced, the people instructed to discountenance them, and the Bishops ordered to prevent them from preaching or holding meetings in their wards. Taking it at its incipiency, by vigorous measures Brigham succeeded in crushing out the organization.

Next was a party of seceders headed by John Morris, in 1860-61. The Morrisites became more numerous than the Gladdenites, and some of them still exist, though they, too, were pretty well crushed out at the time of the fight to which I before alluded when speaking of the murder of their leader.

In 1863 the most threatening movement in opposition to the Brigham dynasty took place. It was the preaching of anti-polygamous Mormonism by the disciples of Joseph Smith, son of the first Prophet. Joseph claims to be the head of the Mormon Church, and his followers known as the Josephites, and to these I have before alluded, also.

In 1863 Smith sent two missionaries from Nauvoo to Zion; and notwithstanding the opposition of Brigham Young, they went about preaching from house to house, and in one winter obtained several hundred converts to their branch of Mormonism, the majority of whom went back to the States with the missionaries the following summer. Smith is preparing for a more extensive missionary work in Utah next summer.

The slightest movement that threatens a loss of faith in Brigham is denounced and discouraged in every possible way. The Josephites are now his particular hatred, and he declares such apostates to be "worse than those who damn the Mormons and all Mormonism."

What I have already submitted is evidence that the people may be convinced of their error, and the difficulty all lies in reaching them with the truths of Christianity. To elevate and save the immoral and degraded is a duty of the Christian Church! To prevent and punish crime is a duty of the Government! Brigham Young will interpose every obstacle he may be capable of bringing in the way, to thwart both in the discharge of these duties, but they may all be overcome by a judicious and systematic course. If churches are built for public worship, Brigham will not allow his saints to attend them. If the missionary visits the people from house to house, those who entertain him will be marked, and perhaps punished. The people will be publicly and privately cautioned to hold no fellowship with missionaries, and Sabbath-schools will be discountenanced. These are some of the influences that will operate against the success of a missionary enterprise; but where is there a mission in this or foreign land that has not encountered similar difficulties?

There are several encouraging features that will be connected with an attempt to enlighten the Mormons. Not least among them is the influx of a Gentile population into the territory, and in this there is a very decided advantage gained. The mere contact of the two classes will have a wonderful effect in showing the moral, religious and physical advantages of a different life. Then another feature is that the Government is committed to put down polygamy, and in doing so the Church will obtain the important ally which I have said was so necessary to secure tolerance. A regard for the rights of individuals, rigidly required by United States civil officers, with a military force to compel respect, would secure this. Brigham Young may be defiant now, but when he finds his people emerging from their present moral and political darkness, and contending only for such rights and privileges as conform to the genius of our institutions, and he sees the Government determined to protect them in these rights, his influence will have waned. He then cannot cry "persecution and intolerance," as he has so often done, for it will be manifest to the people that the Government is protecting them from the persecution and intolerance of a most intolerant leader.

The time for the Church so take her stand and make use of these aids, is now fast approaching. The completion of the Pacific Railroad will usher in the fullness of that time. If she fails to improve it, the responsibility for a continuance of the present state of society in Utah, and perhaps of strife and bloodshed that may follow, will to some extent at least rest upon her. Such opportunities as the present are not often presented. I believe that nowhere will more willing converts to true Christianity be found than among the more sincere of the Mormons; and their enlightenment is more especially desirable because of their aggressive work in error. They are in this respect different from any other people among whom missionaries are sent to labor. Their errors are not only inculcated upon their children, and the sect increased by the multiplication of the people among themselves by natural laws, but hundreds and thousands are being led into error and added to their number every year, and numbers of women hopelessly degraded by their practice of polygamy.

A minister in a prominent church in Washington once remarked in a missionary sermon to his congregation that the missionaries of "our rougher brethren," the Methodists, are as the frontiersmen who cut down the forests, while they followed on to grub out the stumps and cultivate the fields; and again, he compared the former to the reapers in the field, while the more refined followed on, and gathered the scattering grain that the reapers had not bound in their sheaves. If this minister's ideas of the labors that pertained to certain branches of the Church are correct, then it is to "our rougher brethren," particularly, that these remarks should be addressed. Let their frontiersmen or their reapers go forth into Utah, and I would accept the latter simile as the most applicable in this case, for instead of a forest primeval to be levelled, are fields of error fertilized and cultivated, now all white unto harvest, awaiting the scythe of the reaper. There is work for both reaper and gleaner. But the first great work should not be confined to a denomination of Christians, but on it all the Churches should unite their influences. That work is to secure the coöperation of the Government with the Church.

The Rev. Mr. McLeod, of the Congregational Church, to whom I have before referred as the chaplain at Camp Douglas, who has done good in Salt Lake City, is now absent in the States, lecturing against Mormonism, and collecting funds for building a church. Something more than the enterprise of one minister is required, and unsupported he can do but little—less than when he held a commission as chaplain. Moreover, though Mr. McLeod may be admirably suited for the work in other respects, his expositions and denunciations of Mormonism have made him so obnoxious to the people as, in my opinion, to interfere with the usefulness which otherwise his talents and energy would insure.

Before concluding this already too long chapter on such a subject by such a writer, I must add a few words on the abolition of polygamy. Referring to the writer, it is but justice to such officers to say that he is not a chaplain. That may have been patent to most of the readers, but not to all.

The provision to be made for surplus wives is a subject that requires thoughtful attention, in connection with the abolition of polygamy. If the present law could be so construed as to be prospective in its requirements, and forbid the future marrying of more than one wife, and not apply to those who had a plurality of wives before its passage to put away all but their lawful wife, I think the evil could be as effectually remedied in a few years. This would also increase the opportunities of the Church in elevating the standard of morality, at the same time that it labored to satisfy the people that their church taught not only a political evil, but a social, moral and natural one.

Polygamy has already degraded the woman, and for her to continue as a duplicate wife until circumstances provided a way for her to change her relation, I consider by far preferable to compelling the man to put her away to become the subject of a public or a private charity.

CHAPTER XXI.

THE INDIANS OF THE PLAINS AND MOUNTAINS.

THE several tribes of Indians living on the prairies, and in the mountains of the West, are so similar in their habits, and in their general traits of character, that I may not improperly speak of them all as one people, and refer to any peculiarities of a single tribe that may occur to me as I write.

The tribes that came under my personal observation during the march, of which I have given some account in this work, were respectively the Ottoe, Pawnee, Sioux, Cheyenne, Utes and Shoshones. The first named is but the remnant of a tribe now living on an Indian reservation in Kansas. They are supposed to be more nearly civilized than the others, being thrown in contact with more whites, and to a very limited extent cultivate the soil. They have not been hostile for a long time.

The Pawnees have also been greatly decimated by their conflicts with the Sioux, who were vastly their superiors in numbers, though for gallantry and skill in Indian warfare they did not surpass their unfortunate enemies. The Pawnees also occupy a reservation in the eastern part of Nebraska, and may be no longer regarded as among the hostile Indians of the plains.

The Sioux and Cheyenne roam over the prairies, bordering the mountains, and up into them, and the former claim as their favorite hunting ground a portion of Dakota Territory, through which the Government has established, and is endeavoring to protect an emigrant route. This they refuse to give up, and in a large council at Fort Laramie last June, no advantageous treaty for the possession of that country could be made.

The Sioux tribe is the largest on the plains, and their hostilities to emigrants since the failure of the Indian Commission to treat with them satisfactorily on the occasion referred to, will probably result in another Indian war next summer.

The tribe is divided into seven principal bands, who roam from Minnesota to the Rocky Mountains, but each in a somewhat circumscribed locality which they claim as their own hunting-ground. In consequence of this division of the tribe they sometimes call themselves the Seven Council Fires. They have proved the most dangerous enemies the white man has among the savages of the West. In 1854 they massacred Lieutenant Grattan, and thirty men, without leaving a man of his party to tell of the massacre; and in the winter of 1866-7 Brevet Lieutenant-Colonel Fetterman, Captain Brown and Lieutenant Grummond, with over ninety men, shared a similar fate at the hands of the same tribe, and such other Indians as had united with them for murder and robbery.

The Utes range in and west of the Rocky Mountains, from Bridger Pass as far west as Salt Lake City, and then southward to New Mexico. The Shoshone (or Snake) tribe have their favorite hunting-ground in the Wind River Valley, and travel south and west during the summer months. These two tribes are now at peace with the white man, and receive their annual presents from the Government. Only three years ago the Snakes were at war with the troops stationed in Utah, but after a severe battle on Bear River, in which they were severely punished, and sustained a great loss, they in the dead of winter, and in an almost starving condition, begged for peace, and for subsistence. When they arrayed themselves against the white men in the territory, it was in opposition to the advice of their chief Washiki, who is the finest specimen of an Indian I ever saw. He abandoned the leadership of the tribe, rather than indulge in a war which he knew must prove disastrous to the red man. In their folly they elected another chief, and paid for it in the disaster to which I alluded. During the war, Washiki, with his squaws and a small party, camped in the vicinity of Fort Bridger, and after its termination the tribe were only too glad to reinstate him in his former official position.

The general appearance of the Indian, and his physique, are too well understood to justify a description of them here. I must add, however, that in stature and in physical strength he fell far below my expectations. The Indians of the West, who go to Washington on business with the Indian Bureau, or to visit their "Great Father," and the noble-looking figures which appeared in Mr. Stanley's collection of paintings, destroyed by fire in the Smithsonian Institute a few years ago, are by no means representatives of the masses to which I have just alluded. I have seen but one Indian, Washiki, in all my travels, who could be classed with such as I referred to. In physical strength and muscular development they are much the inferior of the average of white men, and will never encounter them in single combat.

Let me write first about the squaws, though they are of the degraded sex, as I have so much to say about their "lords," who are better known in western parlance as "bucks," that I might occupy all the space allowed for this chapter without referring to them.

The beauty of the squaws, as I have observed them, is all a myth. I have yet to see one bearing the slightest comparison in point of beauty with Pocahontas as she is described and painted. I found the large majority of them exceed ingly homely and many horribly ugly. This is the case particularly with the old women, some of whom have the most unsightly faces I ever saw on human forms; and to make their appearance still more disgusting, are their filthy persons and habits. They have no incentive to be otherwise, for they are the most complete slaves of the men (not the old squaws only, but all), and are required to do all manner of drudgery. They dress and tan skins, prepare and dry game, put up and take down lodges, transport them on the animals they ride, catch and saddle the ponies of the men, and in a word, do everything but hunt and fight. They are not easily distinguished from the men at a distance, when their features cannot be observed, and, indeed, many times I have been unable to distinguish them by their features, or in any other way, as the outer dress of both is alike—a buffalo-skin or a blanket. They are generally shorter and broader than the men, and formed not unlike the negress. The dress of the female consists in an unnameable garment, extending from the neck to the knees, open under each arm nearly to the waist, and not in front or behind, which seems rather inconvenient when nursing their children; a pair of short leggins, the moccasin, and the robe or blanket. They ride in the same manner that men do. Both sexes have their heads uncovered, as a rule, though sometimes the men wear old hats obtained from soldiers or immigrants, and both wear their hair long, which is invariably thick and black.

The women, particularly, discard all covering for their heads except their robes, or blankets. These they pull over them in the same way the men do. I have seen squaws who have left their tribes, to live with white men, who have been dressed like ladies in every other respect, but refuse, under all circumstances, "a love of a bonnet;" and though they may wear a fine delaine dress and cashmere shawl, the latter will be pulled up to answer instead of a hat.

The squaws carry their pappooses in a variety of contrivances. Some fold their blankets in a way to form a bag on their back, large enough to hold the offspring in an upright position, with its head out; others have a leather or skin pouch, in which the babe is carried, hung to the back of his mother; and others carry them in the same position, in a case of bark or dried stiff skins, with only an opening over the face. This contrivance resembles a metallic burial-case more than anything else I can think of now.

When the hopeful cries, the mother pacifies it by swaying herself from side to side, or back and front. Walking or riding, as a rule, they are carried on the back, but I have seen a pappoose, in a skin pouch, suspended from the pommel of a saddle, like a pistol and holster. It is a common thing for an Indian mother to make a long journey, and carry her infant in some one of these ways when it is only a few days old.

When the mother gives birth to her child it is not uncommon for no third person to be present. She then lives in a hut, or lodge, by herself, until the child is twenty-five or thirty days old, when she takes it to its father, who then sees his child for the first time. Chastity is observed by the young squaw and guarded by the mother, because it increases the chances of her becoming the wife of a "big Indian," rather than from any moral restraint. Infidelity is not common among wives, and when it occurs is often followed by severe punishment to both guilty parties. The lover may be slain, but it is not uncommon to appease the anger of the injured husband by the present of a pony or other valuable gift.

Indian children of a few years, of both sexes, I think, are more attractive in appearance than when they become older. They are generally treated very kindly, and soon become "spoiled children" in the fullest sense of the word. When a youngster of six or eight strikes his father it is regarded as a hopeful sign of coming bravery, and is spoken of accordingly. The boys are early taught that their mother is to be their slave.

The men are hunters and warriors only. They consider it degrading to the sex to do any kind of manual labor. I think there is combined with this pride a laziness, which, of itself, might account for their habits as long as they have their women with them to do the work. This, they think, is her sphere of life. I was amused one day at the conduct of an intelligent and rather fine-looking warrior, when asked by one of the ladies in our party if he loved his wife. The fellow understood and spoke English. The idea seemed quite absurd to him, and laughing and shaking his head, he turned to his father-in-law, who was sitting next to him, and said something very amusing to him also, probably that the pale-faced women were big fools to think of their sex being loveable creatures.

The men and boys are all good riders and prize their ponies very highly, though their ill-treatment of the animals seem rather inconsistent with real fondness for them. Their sporting arms and war weapons are of great variety, from the Henry repeating rifles and Colt's revolvers to their primitive weapons, the bow and arrow and the lance. The large majority are armed only with the latter. In their hands the bow and arrow is decidedly the most effective, and these they use with great skill, shooting their arrows in rapid succession, with remarkable accuracy, and a force that will send them entirely through the body of a buffalo. The arrows are sometimes poisoned, for war purposes, by the tribes east of the mountains. This is done by touching their tips in the poison of the rattle-snake, and some vegetable poison they also use for the purpose, but I have been unable to ascertain what it is. Their bows vary in size. The Indians who always go mounted, have short ones, say three feet long, while some of the tribes in the West, who fight on foot, have them nearly twice as long. Each tribe makes its arrows of a particular kind of wood, or in a peculiar way, so that the tribe can be told by its arrows.

Scalping is still practiced among all the tribes, and not only the warrior who is slain in battle, but the lonely Indian hunter or the poor immigrant, who falls by an arrow from the bow of his wily foe, have their bodies mutilated in the same way. Nor are the dead only subjected to this barbarous practice, but a wounded enemy is scalped when he is supposed to have a mortal wound, or one such may be given him after the process. Sometimes these wounds do not prove fatal, and the injured party recovers, minus a slice of the skin and hair along the top of his head. The most approved way of scalping is to take only a small piece of skin from the occiput, to which the "scalp-lock" is attached. I saw a fresh scalp last fall taken by a Ute from an Arrapahoe. The brave who took it seemed to have been rather greedy, as it included the entire skin of the head. It was stretched out on a little hoop of willow, and the squaw of the owner carried it, and appeared to be very careful of the precious property. Whatever size or shape the trophy may be, it must contain the scalp-lock. This is to prevent fraud. If some such precaution were not taken, a dishonest warrior might cut up one into a dozen. Scalps with long hair attached are more highly prized, and used in decorating the person of the brave who owns them. The insignia of rank is often made from these, and consists of portions of the scalp attached to the shoulder, or on the fringe of the leggings, &c.

A "scalp-dance" is no ordinary occasion of rejoicing; it occurs after the warrior returns to his friends with his trophies. If, after a battle, in which some of the tribe may have been killed, the mourning of the relatives is turned into rejoicing, at the evidence of revenge for their slain, and all are merry alike. The scalps not used as ornaments are carefully preserved by the owners as evidence of their prowess, and if at any time a dispute as to the bravery of a warrior arises, he produces his trophies of battle, or cold-blooded murder, as the case may be.

Chieftainship is not always hereditary, though the son of a "Big Chief," the head of a tribe, is an under-chief by virtue of his birth, but at the death of his father he does not succeed him as the head of the tribe unless he has arrived at proper age, and has exhibited such discretion and valor as to entitle him to the position. Tribes are divided into bands, and over each is a chief; and bands have also their subdivisions, with their chief. At the death of the head of a tribe, the other chiefs select from their number his successor, giving preference to the child-chief, all other qualifications being equal.

The medicine-man is probably, next to the chief, the most important and distinguished member of the tribe to which he belongs. He is doctor, sorcerer, priest, and altogether a wonderful man. For the cure of disease he relies principally upon the laying-on of hands; and I hope, for the benefit of sick savages, he is more successful than the Mormons are in the same practice. These manipulations are made with many gestures, amidst all kinds of sounds on the part of the persons present looking on, as well as the manipulator. They use also certain herb infusions, the principal virtue of which is supposed to be imparted by the ceremony which goes on during the preparation. Some of the tribe treat their diseases indiscriminately by taking a hot steam-bath, and a cold plunge immediately afterward. They construct a little bath-house with twigs, and throw their blankets over it, or put their blankets over their heads, taking some very hot stones under them, pour on the water, which causes the steam to arise, and the perspiration to pour out upon the skin, when they will come out of their steam-baths, which are taken by a stream, and plunge into the cold water.

If the disease can be localized, the most reliable remedy under such circumstances is for the medicine-man to apply his mouth and suck (imagine the shudder of the writer) the skin or diseased part to remove the morbid humors. If the patient is suffering from a wound, that process is almost certainly gone through with. They not unfrequently practice a little chicanery, and work upon the imagination of the patient by producing an insect, or a bit of stone, or almost anything, while they are going through their cantations and manipulations, which they had secreted about their person, and then present it to the patient with the representation that it is the embodiment of the disease that has been extracted from the system. Why isn't this as justifiable and good a practice, as to make people believe tnat they are cured by little sugar-pills marked aconit., belladonna, nux vomica, chinco., etc., upon the miniature vials that contain them. The medicine-men of the Sioux tribe have a sacred language which is unintelligible to the masses. As I said before, the medicine-man is a great deal thought of by the Indians, and they, like people generally with pale faces, are disposed to attribute a good deal of the work of nature to the doctor's remedies.

The tribes I have seen are not the inveterate smokers the nation have the reputation of being, but all seem to indulge, more or less. Pure tobacco is never smoked by the Indian, and with many no tobacco at all, but the dry bark of the young willow-tree. Their kilikinnik is supposed to consist of a mixture of one-third tobacco and the remainder of willow-bark or dried sumach leaves. I find the addition of these substances in smaller proportions is a great improvement to the ordinary smoking tobacco, according to my taste.

The Indian smokes differently from the white man, and inhales the fumes into his lungs, hence he cannot tolerate the pungency of our tobacco. I have seen three or four coughing and contorting their faces after a puff or two from the pipe of an officer, who passed it to them as an evidence of friendship.

The Indian is not named in childhood, but assumes a name as he grows up for some distinguishing feat or peculiar characteristic, and changes it from time to time as more fitting ones are suggested. Some of their names are very odd and some quite obscene.

The wife is sometimes "wooed and won," as if there was something of sentiment in the Indian character, but oftener purchased without the wooing. When the desired object is particularly attractive, and of a good family, the courting and purchasing both may be required. Indians are polygamists, and when a brave or chief desires to multiply the number of his wives he often marries several sisters, if they can be had, not because of any particular fancy he may have for any but the one who first captivated him, but because he thinks it more likely to have harmony in the household when they are all of one family. Not even squaws can live happily together when each may have a part interest in the man as their husband jointly. Polygamy is inconsistent with the female character, whether in barbarism or civilization. As many skins as they can transport on their ponies, of the game killed while on their hunts, are dressed by the squaws and then taken to some trading-post, a military station, or elsewhere, and bartered off for such articles as are most useful to them; and I am sorry to say that powder, lead and caps, too often, and in too large quantities, are the articles traded for. They are willing to allow much more, proportionately, for ammunition, than any other articles. Buffalo robes, bear-skins, and deer and antelope skins, are the ones they generally bring in, though some of the tribes trap or shoot the beaver, otter, etc., expressly for their furs.

The Indian dead are disposed of in several ways. Some of the tribes, the Sioux among them, place the body on an elevated platform in an unfrequented place; others bury it in the ground, and others hide it in crevices of the rocks, &c. All that pertained to the dead, while living, in the way of robes, blankets, weapons, cooking utensils, &c., are also deposited with the body. In some instances the horse is buried with the dead body of his former rider placed in the saddle. They believe that the spirit of the deceased wanders off to distant hunting-grounds; and as it may have to pass over a country where there is no game, a quantity of dried buffalo meat is usually left with the body for its subsistence while on the journey. With tribes that do not bury horse and rider together, a horse belonging to the deceased is usually shot that his spirit may not have to go afoot a long journey to his new hunting-ground. A gentlemen informed me that recently he was passing a camp of the Snakes, when he saw three of their finest horses shot, and upon inquiring why it was done, learned that an Indian who had owned them died the night before. When a married brave dies, his squaw subjects herself to all manner of torture as evidence of the sincerity of her grief. They often lacerate their bodies in the most horrid manner, and subject themselves to various other kinds of suffering. The squaw, like her sex generally, is proud of her hair, but on such occasions it is cut close to the head. The tribes that bury their dead are careful to leave nothing that would indicate a grave, though the friends observe landmarks by which they can ever afterward tell the exact spot where they lie. These places of sepulture are held as sacred as a Christian nation's, and when a tribe is again passing such localities, they will make a détour, rather than go the more direct road, by the resting-place of their dead, while the relatives leave the trail and go alone to the spot, and there repeat their mourning as if in the presence of the departed. They also leave their presents for the dead of such little trinkets as he most prized before he departed to his new hunting-ground. How beautiful this practice of a barbarous nation, which savors so much of the finer sensibilities of the most enlightened!

The Indians are almost universally fond of whiskey, and have a strong propensity for gambling. They will risk at cards almost everything they own, and if unsuccessful appear quite satisfied with their loss. I wonder if there is something in the atmosphere of the Far West that makes gambling so general. Upon that hypothesis I might account for the habits of a good many of my pale-faced friends.

The Indians have a peculiar way of defining time. When they wish to designate an hour of the day they point to the position the sun should be in at that time. The number of days is the number of sleeps. Ask a Shoshone how far it is from Salt Lake City to Fort Bridger, and he will place the side of his head upon the palm of his hand, signifying sleep, and hold up four fingers, meaning that number of days or sleeps will be passed on the journey. Their next division of time is the number of moons, instead of our months, and the seasons are indicated by the state of vegetation, &c. For instance, spring is when the grass begins to grow, and autumn when the leaves fall from the trees, while the years are indicated as the number of seasons.

There is a language of signs common to all the tribes, by which one tribe may communicate with another, without being able to speak or understand its dialect. Each tribe is known by some particular sign. The Pawnee, called by some the Wolf Tribe, are known by the sign of placing by the side of the head the two forefingers of the right hand, representing a wolf's ears. The Cheyenne, or Cut Wrists, are known by the sign of drawing the edge of their hand across the left wrist; the Sioux, or Cut-Throats, by drawing the edge of the hand across the throat; the Utes have a complicated sign denoting "Living in the Mountains;" the Shoshone, or Snake Tribe, by making a motion similar to that made by the snake.

The principal diet of the Indians of the West is meat, which they obtain by hunting wild game, and eat it fresh in season or where it abounds, and dry it for use when away from their hunting-grounds. They also make use of some varieties of wild vegetables, but none of the tribes that I have named cultivate the soil. They by no means despise many articles of the white man's diet. Of coffee they are fond, but sugar they prefer to eat alone and undissolved, and seem to regard it as a very great delicacy.

The Indian is noted for his powers of endurance, of both fatigue and physical pain. A gentleman recently cited to me a remarkable example of the latter, which he witnessed near Fort Laramie last summer. The representatives of a large number of tribes had collected there, with a view to enacting the farce of a treaty. When riding out near the post one day, he observed a large collection of Indians apparently enjoying very much some exhibition that was then taking place, and upon approaching the spot he saw Indians inflicting upon themselves the severest torture to prove their fitness to rank as warriors of the tribe. The process was this: a buck Indian would gather up in one hand as much of the skin and flesh as he could grasp over the pectoral muscle (the large muscle on the side of the chest) and then transfix it with a knife, making an incision large enough to pass in a stout stick; to this stick was attached a rope with the other end fastened to the top of a pole set in the ground. When this was done the Indian would pull back until he tore out the stick through the skin and flesh, and if unable to accomplish it by a steady pull, he would forcibly throw himself backward, hoping by a sudden jerk to overco me the resistance of the tissues. The friend who observed all this represented that in one instance the savage had transfixed the muscle so deeply as to be unable, without assistance to tear it through, so he had his pony fastened to him, and made to pull until he was liberated; when his conduct was applauded by the loudest shouts of his companions. After subjecting themselves to this ordeal, they ranked higher in the tribe, and seemed very proud of their new honor.

Captain Burton, when he visited the Far West in 1860, in speaking of the power of endurance in the Indian, says: "their fortitude and endurance of pain is the result, as in the prize-fighter, of undeveloped brain." If the Captain should again visit this country, and be invited to the floor of the House of Representatives, he might not be very cordially received by all its members.

There are things connected with the habits of the Indian I might mention, but I have already extended this chapter longer than I intended, and I must now add something about his character and conduct toward the whites who chance to be in his country.

"The noble red man" is a prolific subject for the novelist, who knows nothing about his real character, and the "Poor Indian" is made to live in song very prejudicial to the character of those who have to deal with him.

The settler in the Far West, and the immigrant journeying across the continent, regard the red-skin in a very different light from the novelist and the poet. I know of but two or three Indians of the Rocky Mountain tribes who are supposed, even by the pseudo-humanitarians in the vicinity of Salt Lake City, to possess a single trait of true nobility. The character of Pocahontas in saving the captive Smith, is so out of keeping with the character of squaws of the present day, that if I regard her as a specimen of her nation, then I must consider the squaws now debased beyond hope of improvement. But it is now made to appear that Captain Smith's story of Pocahontas saving his life was all a fabrication, and that she possessed none of the remarkable feelings of kindness, or any other of the good traits generally attributed to her; that she was a common indecent squaw, perhaps of more than ordinary attractiveness of appearance, and lionized in England after she became the wife of an Englishman.

The Indian does everything through motives of policy. He has none of the kindlier feelings of humanity in him. He is as devoid of gratitude as he is hypocritical and treacherous. He observes a treaty or promise only so long as it is dangerous for him to disregard it, or for his interest, in other ways, to keep it. His selfishness is unequalled by any other people, and is often manifested in the most unnatural ways. For instance: when a tribe is moving, a "buck" may have two or three extra horses running loose, but he will not allow a brother, or sister, or mother, to ride one of them, though they may be journeying afoot. Cruelty is inherent in them, and is early manifested in the young pappoose torturing birds, or any little animal that may fall into his hands, and he seems to delight in it; while the pleasure of the adult in torturing his prisoners is most unquestionable.

These are usually inflicted by the squaws, because it is supposed to be more mortifying and humiliating to be tortured by a woman. They are inveterate beggars, but never give unless with a view to receive a more valuable present in return, and then their's is likely to be reclaimed. Hence we hear our children say, "I wouldn't make an Indian gift." They lie from principle, as it were. To sum up the whole in a word, they possess every trait of human character that is despicable, and no trait that is noble.

The white man he has been taught is his enemy, and he has become the most implacable enemy of the white man. His most fiendish murders of the innocent is his sweetest revenge for a wrong that has been done by another.

At Fort Laramie, last summer, as I have before stated, there was an Indian Commission sent out by authority of the Interior Department at Washington, to treat with the Sioux and other hostile tribes. The president of the Commission was a Quaker gentleman with a heart overflowing with the milk of human kindness, and he went there, as he said, to fight the Indian with a new weapon—"Christian love." To those who understand the Indian character, and saw of what material the commission was composed, it was evident what would be the result of the grand council which had been so much talked about on the plains; and what has been the result? It is certainly not very encouraging to the commission. There have been more murders by the Indians of the tribe represented in that council than ever before occurred in the same length of time. Unprotected immigrants have been massacred; telegraph stations destroyed, and the operators and guard made to share the same fate as the immigrant; five officers of the U. S. Army, and nearly one hundred and fifty men, have been murdered; and the life of an individual is not safe outside the stockades of the forts in the country the commission came to treat for the possession of.

Who were the Indians that met at Laramie on the occasion of the treaty? The best authorities represent that they were the old men, squaws, and their children, who made it an occasion for eating Government rations and drinking sutler whiskey, while the warriors of the tribes were out hunting and plundering, so as to secure a sufficient stock of necessaries preparatory to open hostilities that were to follow. An idea of the spirit manifested by even those who had assembled, might have been formed when an old chief comes forward with a pipe in one hand and a bow and arrow in the other, and offers to Colonel Maynadier, the commanding officer, his choice, perfectly defiant, meaning, if the Indian could have what he wanted they would smoke together, but if he could not, then they would fight.

The terms of the fruitless treaty I have not learned; but the Indians persisted in retaining the Powder River country as their hunting-ground, while an emigrant route had already been opened through it, and forts established. Extensive presents were made to conciliate the Indian, who would not treat satisfactorily. They recovered the blankets, clothing, hatchets, etc., that were given to them, as evidence that the white man was afraid of them; and the butcher-knives which were included in the presents, were found very useful and efficient by slightly perverting their use, and scalping immigrants within a hundred miles of the post, two months after the adjournment of the council. By authority of the commission, the Indians were allowed to purchase or trade for powder of the sutler, whose stock was soon exhausted, but afterward replenished from the nearest point—Denver City—and that too disposed of. This was probably the new mode of fighting with "Christian love." It certainly furnished the Indians with the means of fighting much more effectively.

It is the purpose of the Government to protect the emigrant to the western territory; but the temporizing policy of the Interior Department has so trammeled the War Office, as to defeat the ends which the Government desire to attain. A more decisive course will doubtless soon be inaugurated. At the date of this writing the House of Representatives have passed a bill transfering the Indian Bureau to the War Department, and there is but little doubt of the concurrence of the Senate and the approval of the President.

General Sherman in his annual report, which was written before the Fort Phil. Kearney massacre, declared his intention to confine the several tribes to certain specified localities, and if an Indian is found outside his proper limits, without a pass, he is to be "summarily punished," which I construe to mean he will be shot. And again: when referring to the murder of Lieutenant Daniels, of the 18th Infantry, and a few soldiers who were the only parties killed up to that time, he says "their death must be avenged next summer." General Sherman is not noted for using idle words for effect! Since his report was sent in the atrocities have been increased ten-fold, which will doubtless result in a ten-fold sterner policy on the part of that distinguished officer, more particularly if the Bureau is made a part of the War Department, for in his report he seems fearful lest he should come in conflict with some of the treaties of the Secretary of the Interior. He does not, however, hesitate to forbid the sale of arms to Indians when the Indian Commissioner has authorized it.

The reader can well imagine the disgust of officers on the frontier, after learning the particulars of the massacre of our personal friends, when we read in the newspaper telegrams from the Commissioner of Indian Affairs discrediting the published accounts of the outrage; and when forced to believe them, other telegrams, to the effect that there must have been some *misunderstanding*, or the Indian would not have been so naughty; and then again, others that he has requested an investigation into the matter by Congress *that justice may be done to the Indian* as well as the military. How decidedly cool, when the lives of hundreds and thousands are in jeopardy because of the confidence imparted to the savages by their success in the fearful massacre which the Indian Bureau would justify if possible.

It is my opinion that the present generation of Indians can be taught but little idea of moral obligations; that they cannot be christianized, as at present situated; and the only alternative remaining is to punish them for their crimes, and keep them in constant fear of further punishment, if they dare offend, until the settlers in the Indian country become sufficiently numerous to defend themselves.

THE END.

FATHER TOM AND THE POPE; OR, A NIGHT IN THE VATICAN. With a Preface and Ante-Preface by FRED'K S. COZZENS. Cloth, 75c. Sent free by mail on receipt of price.

GALILEO: HIS LIFE, HIS DISCOVERIES AND HIS WORKS. Translated from the French of Dr. Max. Parchappe, by HUON D'ARAMIS. This biography of one of the most celebrated men the world has produced, has been pronounced, by European critics, to be the best ever written. Dr. Max. Parchappe, the author, died, just as he had completed a work which will long remain a monument of his erudition and impartiality.

SLAVE SONGS OF THE UNITED STATES. Set to Music. A new edition of this popular work is just issued. Cloth, $1.50. Sent free by mail on receipt of price.

The Press says of it:

"We welcome the volume before us—the first collection of negro songs, words and music, that has been made."—*N. Y. Independent.*

"They have no sort of resemblance to the so-called negro songs of the corked minstrels, and, as a rule, are much more attractive."—*N. Y. Citizen.*

"The verses are expressive, and the melodies touching and effective. There is no doubt the book will receive wide attention."—*Brooklyn Standard.*

"Possesses a curious interest for the student of African character."—*N. Y. Tribune.*

"These endemical lays are, in fact, chief among the signs and evidences of the normal African character."—*N. Y. World.*

"This collection contains many excellent ballads that might readily be supposed the work of our best composers."—*Le Messager Franco-Americain.*

THE GLAD NEW YEAR, AND OTHER POEMS. By ETHEL WOLF.

A very attractive volume. Sent free by mail on receipt of price. Cloth, $1.25.

LIFE AMONG THE MORMONS; A JOURNEY TO THE CITY OF ZION. BY A U. S. OFFICER NOW LIVING IN UTAH. One of the most interesting and readable books ever issued on polygamy, and the doings of the Saints.

Cloth, $1.25. Sent free by mail on receipt of price.

THE DARTROUS DIATHESIS, OR ECZEMA AND ITS ALLIED AFFECTIONS. By A. HARDY, M.D., Physician to the St. Louis Hospital, Paris. Translated by HENRY G. PIFFARD, M.D., late House Surgeon Bellevue Hospital; Physician to the Skin Department, Out-Door Bureau, Bellevue Hospital; Assistant to Chair of Theory and Practice, Bellevue Hospital Medical College. Sent free by mail on receipt of price. Cloth, $1.25. Paper, $1.00.

A TREATISE ON

EMOTIONAL DISORDERS OF THE SYMPATHETIC SYSTEM OF NERVES. By WM. MURRAY, M.D., etc., Physician to the Dispensary, and to the Hospital for Sick Children, and Lecturer on Physiology in the College of Medicine, Newcastle-on-Tyne. Second American edition. Cloth, $1.50. Sent free by mail on receipt of price.

FELIX VON NIEMEYER'S CLINICAL LECTURES ON PULMONARY PHTHISIS. Translated by permission of the Author from the second German Edition. By J. L. PARKE. Sent free by mail on receipt of price. Cloth, $1.50. Paper, $1.25.

HYSTERIA.—REMOTE CAUSES OF DISEASE IN GENERAL. TREATMENT OF DISEASE BY TONIC AGENCY. LOCAL OR SURGICAL FORMS OF HYSTERIA, etc. Six Lectures delivered to the Students of St. Bartholomew's Hospital, 1866. By F. C. SKEY, F.R.S.

The well-known ability and experience of the distinguished author of this work will insure for it the respectful consideration of the Medical Profession. It is truly admirable, both in form and substance, and will doubtless accomplish much good through those who follow its progressive and scientific teachings. Sent free by mail on receipt of price, $1.50.

LIGHT: ITS INFLUENCE ON LIFE AND HEALTH. By FORBES WINSLOW, M.D., etc. This important work is written in the most simple and perspicuous manner, and is one of those contributions to science which all can understand and appreciate. It is, indeed, a charming treatise on a subject of vital interest. Sent free by mail on receipt of price. Cloth, $1.75.

ON CHRONIC ALCOHOLIC INTOXICATION. With an inquiry into the influence of the Abuse of Alcohol, as a predisposing Cause of Disease. By W. MARCET, M.D., F.R.S., Fellow of the Royal College of Physicians, etc., etc. In convenient size, large type. Sent free by mail on receipt of price. Cloth, $1.75.

PATHOLOGICAL ANATOMY OF THE FEMALE SEXUAL ORGANS. By Prof. JULIUS KLOB, of Vienna. Translated by Drs. J. KAMMERER and B. F. DAWSON. First volume, containing the Diseases of the Uterus. Cloth, $3.50. Sent free by mail on receipt of price.

THE PRINCIPLES AND PRACTICE OF LARYNGOSCOPY AND RHINOSCOPY in Diseases of the Throat and Nasal Passages. Designed for the use of Physicians and Students. With 59 Engravings on Wood. By ANTOINE RUPPANER, M.D., M.A., member of the American Medical Association; of the Massachusetts Medical Society; of the County Medical Society of New York, etc.

Sent free by mail on receipt of price. $2.00.

www.ingramcontent.com/pod-product-compliance
Lightning Source LLC
LaVergne TN
LVHW050513100826
845148LV00002B/320